William Shakespeare: The Tragedies

Twayne's English Authors Series

Arthur F. Kinney, Editor

University of Massachusetts, Amherst

TEAS 415

THE
Tragicall Historie of
HAMLET
Prince of Denmarke

By William Shake-speare.

As it hath beene diuerse times acted by his Highnesse ser
uants in the Cittie of London : as also in the two V
niuersities of Cambridge and Oxford, and else-where

At London printed for N.L. and Iohn Trundell.
1603.

William Shakespeare: The Tragedies

By Paul A. Jorgensen

University of California, Los Angeles

TWAYNE PUBLISHERS
An Imprint of Simon & Schuster Macmillan

Prentice Hall International
London • Mexico City • New Delhi • Singapore • Sydney • Toronto

William Shakespeare:
The Tragedies

Paul A. Jorgensen

Twayne Publishers
An Imprint of Simon & Schuster Macmillan
1633 Broadway
New York, NY 10019-6785

Book Production by Elizabeth Todesco
Book Design by Barbara Anderson

Printed on permanent/durable acid-free
paper and bound in the United States of America.

Library of Congress Cataloging in Publication Data
Jorgensen, Paul A.
   William Shakespeare: the tragedies.

   (Twayne's English authors series; TEAS 415)
   Bibliography: p. 149
   Includes index.
   1. Shakespeare, William, 1564–1616—Tragedies.
I. Title. II. Series
PR2983.J67 1985   822.3'3   85-8587
ISBN 0-8057-6906-4

To Virginia, my wife,
for help and encouragement

Contents

Editor's Note

In this remarkably succinct, often original, frequently witty, and always stimulating study of Shakespeare's ten tragedies from *Titus Andronicus* through *Coriolanus*, Paul A. Jorgensen examines certain key elements each play shares with the others and with its time while concentrating also on Shakespeare's development as a tragic artist and on his unique achievement in each play. For Jorgensen, Shakespearean tragedies finally do not rely on accident, fate, death, or absurdity, but on the self-knowledge that is won by suffering and by the secret of an "open heart." "How one masters the art of known and feeling sorrows is perhaps what a 'tough world' is mainly about"; and in a combination of honesty, nobility, and the power and beauty of language, this is what Shakespeare's major tragic characters—men and women, youth and old age, Roman and Christian and pagan—all learn. By emphasizing their struggles, Shakespeare shows "through 'known and feeling sorrows' the rescue of threatened humanity," a humanity shared by his characters and his audiences, by the Elizabethans and by us. The results of such an investigation can be bold yet persuasive, such as the argument here for a ministering scourge in *Hamlet*, the masterful design of *Timon of Athens*, and the use of silence in *Julius Caesar* and *Antony and Cleopatra* as well as in *Macbeth* and *King Lear*. Jorgensen's original study will alike instruct both new and seasoned students of Shakespeare.

—Arthur F. Kinney

About the Author

Paul A. Jorgensen, Ph.D. from the University of California, Berkeley, is professor of English at the University of California, Los Angeles. A Guggenheim Fellow, his specialty is Shakespeare and the Renaissance. Service on editorial advisory committees of professional journals has helped him keep abreast of scholarship on Shakespeare. These committees include those for *Publication of the Modern Language Association of America* (where he has evaluated up to a hundred submissions a year), *Huntington Library Quarterly, College English,* and *Film Quarterly*. He has done omnibus surveys of scholarship for *Studies in English Literature* and *Texas Studies in Literature and Language*. For five years he served as bibliographer of the Shakespeare Association of America and editor of its *Annual International Shakespeare Bibliography*. He has also published articles in such journals as *English Literary Renaissance, PMLA, Studies in Philology, Modern Language Quarterly, Shakespeare Quarterly, Shakespeare Studies, Journal of the History of Ideas, Clio, Huntington Library Quarterly,* and *Viator*. He has been chairman of the Shakespeare Group of the Modern Language Association of America.

Professor Jorgensen's Shakespeare books include: *Shakespeare's Military World* (Berkeley and Los Angeles: University of California Press, 1956, 1973); *Redeeming Shakespeare's Words* (Berkeley and Los Angeles: University of California Press, 1962); *Othello: An Outline Guide to the Play* (New York: Barnes & Noble, 1964); *Lear's Self-Discovery* (Berkeley and Los Angeles: University of California Press, 1967); and *Our Naked Frailties: Sensational Art and Meaning in "Macbeth"* (Berkeley and Los Angeles: University of California Press, 1971). He also has edited the Pelican edition of *The Comedy of Errors* (New York: Penguin Books, 1964, *et seq.*).

Preface

To turn to the rarefied heights of Shakespeare's tragedies presents both unparalleled challenge and numerous hazards. Because these plays have an accent and a power that are unique and almost unmistakable, there is a temptation for the critic to refer to them as an entity something like a wonder of the world. Such a beholder is likely to call them Shakespearean tragedy, making them a monolithic achievement, towering above other dramatists' works, above other literature, above the era in which they appeared, and even above Shakespeare's other kinds of plays. Having called them Shakespearean tragedy, the critic is sorely tempted to define the term and to approach the plays with a confining thesis.

The present writer, having failed over several years of preparation for this book to encompass all the plays under one theory, is not innocent of applying several approaches that seem to yield meaning to a significant number of the plays. But the differences within the canon—and this is an assured thesis—are not only legion but also a major triumph of the plays. Warily, but also gladly, this volume is called simply *William Shakespeare: The Tragedies*. Without denying the attractiveness of A. C. Bradley's *Shakespearean Tragedy* (limited to four major plays), I will with less valor describe the volume as a study of ten tragedies. These include only those plays generally accepted, by Folio and most scholars, as tragedies and not as English history plays that have tragic aspects, or the unclassifiable *Troilus and Cressida*.

The organization of the book is also simple. These plays, except for *Titus Andronicus* and *Timon of Athens*, can be approximately dated; at least no great error is inevitable in taking them up in the probable order of their writing. To speak of Shakespeare's development in the creation of tragedy is more subject to objection. Though, except for Titus, Shakespeare's heroes and heroines tend to get older (as did the man who played most of the heroes, Richard Burbage), one hesitates to say that as love tragedy *Antony and Cleopatra* is superior to *Romeo and Juliet*; and what improvement can one confidently claim after *King Lear*? There will be less outcry if I view *Titus Andronicus* as an "apprentice piece." But one of his latest tragedies, *Timon of Athens*, must for all its flaws be treated more respectfully. Nevertheless, there is throughout the tragedies more evidence of increasing stature than otherwise. By studying the development of the tragedies in chronological sequence we can at least see workmanship and character becoming more complex.

Before the individual explications, there will be an introductory chapter presenting hypotheses (not firm theses) for the enduring appeal and some of the meaning of the tragedies. The reader will, I hope, accept most of these. In only one proffered approach do I argue for a persistent theme, a theme inadequately pursued by earlier critics. This is a theme almost unavoidable in works so fraught with pain and sorrow. It is what the Renaissance recognized as feeling, and it is so recognized today. Joseph Conrad, for instance, states that as a writer his primary purpose is to make one feel and see; what he says of the reader applies equally to the experience of the character.[1] The suffering of the character can vary from the gentle, preferred sort of humble acceptance described by Edgar in *King Lear* as "known and feeling sorrows" (4.6.218) to the more tumultuous, often heroic agony of what Hamlet calls "towering passion" (5.2.80). Whatever the emotion, according to John Donne, the basest flaw, the lowest and ultimate descent of man, is not to have feeling. Without this feeling we would not have self-discovery; we would not have the deep and usually sympathetic involvement with the character; and, not least of all, we would not have deeply resonant poetry. But let us again stress that this is an approach or hypothesis, not a thesis. So, too, is an awareness of how the characters react to their suffering in the ultimately various plays, for study of characterization is another important, more common approach to the plays, especially now that A. C. Bradley is receiving his deserved respect.

With the exception of a new and strong respect for not only "known and feeling sorrows" but also a positive rather than a negative view of passion, this study may be said to be rooted in some of the more enduring achievements of scholarship. It aims to be "informed," but also to be freshly informed in a way that will revitalize scholarship. Unfortunately, more has been written on the tragedies—perhaps even *Hamlet* alone—than on all of the rest of Shakespeare's plays. Hence, a densely footnoted pastiche of criticism has been avoided in favor of an annotated bibliography. I have more regret in merely summarizing my years of note taking on primary Renaissance sources. I can only assure the reader that, despite fewer quotations, Renaissance thought here presented could in a longer work be more fully documented. The Renaissance ideas and books are simply not permitted to make this volume more of a background Renaissance study than a devotedly close reading of the tragedies themselves.

One final word must be said on behalf of the scope and organization of the volume. There are many, though never adequate, books on Shakespeare's tragedies. This work is one of the few in this time to deal with *all* the tragedies. It is also, I trust, of special value in not slurring the plays by putting three or more in groups, but rather in seeking, in each play, and in terms of itself as well as the canon, that which makes it preeminently Shakespearean: its individual, never duplicated excellence.

Paul A. Jorgensen

University of California, Los Angeles

Acknowledgments

My greatest pleasure comes from acknowledging indebtedness to my students. On all levels, from freshmen to graduates, they have found reading Shakespeare to be a profound influence on their lives. Teachers, too, will be aware of how this knowledge can sustain them, year after year, in the classroom. And it is this knowledge that moved me and helped me to write this book.

I am grateful also for grants from the University Research Committee.

To my typist, Nora Reyes, I am unusually grateful for generous and excellent help.

The frontispiece is a photograph of the title page of the first quarto of *Hamlet* (1603), a priceless possession of the Huntington Library, and here reproduced by their kind permission. The only other copy of this volume exists in the British Library, but this copy lacks the title page.

Abbreviations

Act, scene, and line references are placed in parentheses in the text; for example, (2.4.16–18). All references are to Alfred Harbage, general editor, *William Shakespeare: The Complete Works*, Pelican Text Revised (New York: Viking Press, 1977). In the parenthetical citations, abbreviations of the play titles refer to the following list.

AC	*Antony and Cleopatra*
Ado	*Much Ado about Nothing*
AWW	*All's Well that Ends Well*
AYL	*As You Like It*
CE	*The Comedy of Errors*
Cor	*Coriolanus*
Cym	*Cymbeline*
Ham	*Hamlet*
1H4	*Henry the Fourth, Part I*
2H4	*Henry the Fourth, Part II*
H5	*Henry the Fifth*
1H6	*Henry the Sixth, Part I*
2H6	*Henry the Sixth, Part II*
3H6	*Henry the Sixth, Part III*
H8	*Henry the Eighth*
JC	*Julius Caesar*
KJ	*King John*
Lear	*King Lear*
LLL	*Love's Labour's Lost*
Mac	*Macbeth*
MM	*Measure for Measure*
MND	*A Midsummer Night's Dream*
MV	*The Merchant of Venice*

Chronology of Tragedies

These dates are approximate, but, except for *Titus Andronicus* and *Timon of Athens*, not seriously so. The date given represents that on which the play most likely received its present form. It seldom represents first publication.

1594 *Titus Andronicus*
1596 *Romeo and Juliet*
1599 *Julius Caesar*
1601 *Hamlet*
1604 *Othello*
1605 *King Lear*
1605 *Macbeth*
1606 *Timon of Athens*
1607 *Antony and Cleopatra*
1608 *Coriolanus*

Chapter One

Introduction

Source and Range of Feeling

Although Shakespeare's authentic tragedies all end in death—usually violent and multiple—death is not an adequate source of the emotional power of any of these plays. Nor, for that matter, is the catastrophe itself. Just as Elizabethans were internationally wondered at for their fearlessness—even their indifference to death—so they were uncommonly sensitive to suffering.

Most of them, William Harrison recorded in his *Description of England,* appended to the 1587 edition of Holinshed that Shakespeare so widely used, preferred death to suffering. It is certainly unwise for the modern critic to equate Shakespeare's tragedies with death, or even what causes it. We must be aware, to be sure, of the question of evil, the frequently strong role of villains and accident, all of which lead to the catastrophe. But even the central importance of a catastrophe must be questioned. The substance of the plays is not invariably, or even most probably, to be found in event—intrigue and violent action. Rather it is to be found in the source of the strongest emotion: the ordeal of the hero or heroine and the passion—in its best sense—that the ordeal produces. This passion is most imposing in men of stature. And, as noted, the most heartwrenching language is to be found in men of this sort in—not necessarily mortal—agony. But equally important for tragic effect in Shakespeare is how the protagonist responds to the suffering. The most satisfying response is not stupefaction or even the much admired Stoic elevation, but what Cardinal Wolsey in *Henry VIII* means by "I feel my heart new opened" (3.2.366). But let us look first in more detail at the aspect that may most broadly be called power. Some tragedies by other dramatists may satisfy more when edifying; but none are more powerful than Shakespeare's.

Tragic Stature in Tragic Passion

There could be moderately moving passion without stature. This idea had been pioneeringly demonstrated in Thomas Kyd's *The Spanish Tragedy,* where one of the most common and deeply felt passions, revenge, makes a feeble man, Hieronymo, formidable. And audiences at the popular *Cambyses,* years before, were impressed by the rages of the developing tyranny of the hero. Besides his frightening cruelty, Thomas Preston's hero achieved the illusion of stature by a language that became first admired and then ridiculed. By 1597, Falstaff in his "play extempore" with Prince Hal, suggests the enduring, if cheapening, reputation that this language had: "For I must speak in passion and I will do it in King Cambyses's vein" (*1H4* 2.4.368–69).

But the enduring and genuine union of stature, passion, and language was to come with Christopher Marlowe, notably in *Tamburlaine.* Marlowe's Scythian is truly built on a grand scale:

> Of stature tall, as straightly fashioned,
> Like his desire, lift upwards and divine . . . ,
> Pale of complexion, wrought in him with passion,
> Thirsting with sovereignty, with love of arms,
> His lofty brows in folds do figure death,
> And in their smoothness amity and life.
> Wrapped in curls, as fierce Achilles was. . . .
>   (1 *Tamburlaine* 2.1.7–24)[1]

In passing, it should be noted that, as Reuben Brower has demonstrated, "fierce Achilles" was a model for both the might and the wrath of Elizabethan tragic heroes;[2] and George Chapman, at the beginning of his translation of the *Iliad,* refers to his "banefull wrath."[3] Marlowe's purpose in achieving both stature and passion for Tamburlaine was greatly furthered by his "mighty line," as Ben Jonson phrased it in his commendatory verses to Shakespeare in the First Folio. In the Prologue (1–6), doubtless contrasting his hero and language with such plays as *Cambyses,* Marlowe boasts:

> From jigging veins of rhyming mother wits,
> And such conceits as clownage keeps in pay,
> We'll lead you to the stately tent of war,
> Where you shall hear the Scythian Tamburlaine
> Threat'ning the world with high astounding terms
> And scourging kingdoms with his conquering sword.

Tamburlaine's passions have some range, such as a surprising love for beauty taught him by "suffering" (even though he slaughters virgins), a love of conquest, a pervasively Elizabethan passion for a crown, and his love for Zenocrate. Upon the death of his wife, Tamburlaine is passionate and mighty in a way that the Elizabethan stage had not known before:

> Behold me here, divine Zenocrate,
> Raving, impatient, desperate, and mad,
> Breaking my steeled lance, with which I burst
> The rusty beams of Janus' temple doors,
> Letting out death and tyrannising war,
> To march with me under the bloody flag!
> And, if thou pitiest Tamburlaine the Great,
> Come down from heaven, and live with me again!
> (2 *Tamburlaine*, 2.4.111–18)

The variety of passions rivals, and could distantly have influenced, Shakespeare's Antony with his combination of empire, lust, and grand rage. But Tamburlaine does not progress as a character. He is, like his many imitators, massive but not deeply realized as a human being. Nevertheless, he is the most impressive early exemplar of the potential of passionately achieved grandeur. Marlowe himself makes specific this intention in the running title of part 2, where this passage occurs: "The Second Part of the Bloody Conquests of Mighty Tamburlaine. With his impassionate fury, for the death of his lady and love, fair Zenocrate."

Marlowe's *Edward II* is another pioneering and influential play of passion, but it is about a weak king. He suffers almost as much as any character in Elizabethan tragedy, yet he achieves little sense of impersonal human suffering. And, more important, though the title bears his name, some suggestion as to how Marlowe and his colleagues viewed tragedy is again usefully given in a title: "The troublesome raigne and lamentable death of Edward the second, King of England: with the tragicall fall of proud Mortimer." Edward is "lamentable." Mortimer, a cruel, ambitious, and powerful man, is the real subject of tragedy. He is so also in that he is one of many survivors of the medieval tradition of *de casibus* tragedy. The Elizabethans, with their larger heroes, made especially good use of the "fall of proud men." Mortimer "falls" impressively after both an amorous and ambitious rise; but his fall is almost a triumph. He ridicules the medieval wheel of fortune that takes him down to his death. Instead, he boastfully instructs Queen Isabella to view his death bravely: "Farewell, fair queen; weep not for Mortimer, / That scorns the world, and, as a traveler, / Goes to discover countries yet unknown" (5.6.66–68).

Characters like Mortimer did not come solely from a powerful dramatist like Marlowe. That dauntless, almost aspiring death into an undiscovered country was a vital part of the world in which the dramatists lived. The best known figures were men like Drake, Essex, Raleigh, and Frobisher—and similar to them were even the less glamorous fighting and discovering Englishmen. They were, like Othello, "great of heart" (5.2.361). Because Shakespeare's tragic heroes, to a man, do not express fear of death, another authority on this trait and reputation may be cited. Sir Thomas Smith, in *De Republica Anglorum,* wrote: "In no place shall you see malefactors goe more constantly, more assuredly, and with lesse lamentation [to death] than in England. . . . The nature of our nation is free, stout, haulte, prodigall of life and blood. . . . So that in this nature and fashion our ancient Princes and legislators have nourished them, as to make them stout-hearted, couragious, and souldiers, not villains and slaves."[4] "Prodigall of life and blood" aptly points to a quality that made the kind of tragedy that we know as Shakespearean. And the Dutch Emanuel van Meteren, in *History of the Netherlands* (1599), said of the English: "The people are bold, courageous, ardent, and cruel in war, fiery in attack *(vierlich int aengrijpen),* and having little fear of death; they are not vindictive, but very inconstant, rash, vainglorious."[5] Morever—and this is most important, and most neglected—of the ten tragic heroes whom we shall study, seven are generals or have led armies. Their profession is war, whatever their other occupations or titles may be.

We need for this reason to know something about Essex and Raleigh, not merely because of their valor but also because almost all of this breed were fierce fighters, in war and peace, and even noted for their passionate quarrels, their ambition, and their violent deaths. We could dwell upon Essex, who was described by Sir Francis Bacon in a letter of warning as being "of a nature not to be ruled."[6] We could cite the almost mortal quarrel between him and Raleigh over precedence on the Islands voyage of 1597. And Raleigh, "the best-hated man in England," was not only a genteel courtier; but also, in 1590, in Ireland, he put the Spanish and Italian garrison at Smerwick

to death. Yet of Raleigh further we must be aware not only of his
military cruelty and passion but also of his admirable greatness of
spirit. Spending thirteen years in the Tower, unaware on what day he
would be beheaded, he still wrote a huge folio magnificently hopeless
of completion and typically incautious of design, with an Elizabethan
scope in subject, called *A History of the World.* An especially famous
general, whose last fight was recorded by Raleigh, was Richard Grenville, second in command of a ship called appropriately for the English the *Revenge.* He alone among the English fleet sailed into the
midst of a much larger Spanish armada. He failed, died, and was criticized for being headstrong. According to the Dutch Jan van Linschoten, in *The Fight and Cyclone at Azores,* "he was a man very
unquiet in his minde, and greatly affected to warre. . . . He had performed in many valiant actes, and was greatly feared in these Islands,
and knowne of every man, but of nature very severe, so that his own
people hated him for his fierceness and spoke verie harshly of him."[7]

Raleigh was a literary man, a poet, and had a passion above the
simpler sort that gave him prowess in war. For a fuller picture of the
age, we must turn also to Sir Philip Sidney, a major poet and literary
man, more like Hamlet, who, too, was given a soldier's rites. Sidney
is thus described by Fulke Greville: "Indeed he was a true modell of
Worth, a man fit for conquest, Plantation, Reformation, or whatever
Action soever is greatest and hardest among men."[8] But he was, like
Hamlet, a dangerous man, giving the lie to the powerful Oxford,
who had called him a "puppy." And in a dangerous letter to Sir
Thomas Molyneux, he wrote: "I assure you before God that if ever I
know you do so much as reede any lettre I wryte to my Father, without his commandment, or my consente, I will thruste my Dagger
into you. And truste to it, I speake so in earnest."[9]

To attribute too much of the largeness of valor and passion found
in seven, at least, of Shakespeare's tragic heroes to their military nature would be as incautious as they themselves so grandly were. Yet
the martial nobility of England were notable for these qualities, and,
however dangerous and mortal they might be, these men were proud
of them. As Aufidius says of his enemy Coriolanus, the mighty Roman general could not move "from the casque to the cushion" (*Cor*
4.7.43). He falls prey to lesser men, the tribunes, who plot his
downfall by directing men to

> Put him to choler straight. He hath been us'd
> Ever to conquer, and to have his worth

> Of contradiction. Being once chaf'd, he cannot
> Be rein'd again to temperance. . . .
>
> (3.3.25–28)

These heroes are men of such stature and passion that they tend to meet the awesome, world-shaking end of Antony as prophesied by Charmian: "The soul and body rive not more in parting / Than greatness going off" (*Ant* 4.13.5–6).

These heroes are almost designed to be the noble prey of lesser, craftier creatures. Machiavelli acquainted the English with what men like Raleigh knew only too well: that the successful prince or nobleman must combine the traits of the lion and the fox. "As the lion cannot protect himself from traps," Machiavelli wrote in *The Prince,* "and the fox cannot defend himself from wolves, you have to be a fox to be wary of traps, and a lion to overawe the wolves."[10] Foxes usually prevail in Shakespeare's tragedies, but they could never become tragic heroes.

Yet however imposing these great creatures are in both stature and passion, their size constitutes an unwieldy massiveness in more sophisticated society as their passion leads them to awesome but still mortally wrong choices and to consequent rage and falls. Their usual passion is of course fury, which like the other Aquinan passions comes from pride. But although they cannot be accused of the worst debasement, lack of feeling, their feeling, as we will see, is not always one of beautiful agony. Nor does it, as ire does in *King Lear,* always conduce to nobler insights into self and the world. It does so sometimes when as by a kind of explosion the hero—or certainly the audience—learns the truer hidden nature kept under precarious control.

Just as passions were not by any means limited in Shakespeare to soldiers, so they had a considerable variety. Mostly, we have noted, they were wrathful and vengeful. A few epithets at random: "ireful passion," "strong passion," "towering passion," "tyrannous passion," "bloody passion." Even Romeo, not a soldier but best known as a lover, is described thus by Friar Laurence as the youth offers to slay himself:

> Hold thy desperate hand!
> Art thou a man? Thy form cries out thou art;
> Thy tears are womanish; thy wild acts denote
> The unreasonable fury of a beast.
> Unseemly woman in a seeming man,

> And unseeming beast in seeming both,
> Thou hast amaz'd me!
>
> (*RJ* 3.3.108–14)

Nevertheless, there are, in *Antony and Cleopatra,* passions of love expressed in swelling verse; and in *King Lear* the range of passion produces a thrilling beauty, varying from towering and selfish anger, to bewilderment and deep feeling for others, to the uncertain outcry that ends the play. Passion need not be a merely selfish rage. It could have its older meaning of suffering of almost a religious order, of the kind meant by Bach in "The Passion According to Saint Matthew." Though the reference is only to Thisbe, there is something larger mocked in "her passion ends the play" (*MND* 5.1.308). There is good as well as danger in "Passion lends them power" in *Romeo and Juliet* (Prologue, 13). And though a cruel woman, Tamora in *Titus Andronicus* is speaking from the heart when she pleads: "Victorious Titus, rue the tears I shed, / A mother's tears in passion for her son" (1.1.108–9). Macduff's grief for his country moves Malcolm to believe him: "Macduff, this noble passion, / Child of integrity, hath from my soul / Wiped the black scruples" (*Mac* 4.3.14–16). Antony tells the messenger who hears the report of Caesar's death: "Thy heart is big, get thee apart and weep. / Passion, I see, is catching" (*JC* 3.1.283–84). Moreover, other examples could be cited to show that passion was not viewed always unfavorably as many modern critics have contended. It was a complicated aspect of mankind, as witnessed by the books written then and now on the subject. Most important, though its motive might be selfish, it gave the tragic heroes and heroines not only stature but also poetry and feeling. And surely it is not to condemn its prominence to say that, although most of the books of the age defended it in Christian terms, passion had on the tragic stage as in life rival forms of emotions. These led not to secular grandeur but to a sense of humanity that is less short-lived, less selfish, and ultimately more assuring of man's ability to meet adversity with open heart than the kind of emotion that depended upon a Shakespeare to give it power. And without these rival forms of feeling sorrow there could not be a *King Lear* or a *Hamlet.*

The Art of Known and Feeling Sorrows

An audience, whether in life or in the theater, admires the man or woman who meets adversity with courage (usually passion) or with

patience and felt sorrow. One of the miracles of Shakespeare's tragedies is how we can learn to love, when he suffers, a man whom we
disliked. And one of the central barometers of Shakespeare's characters
is how they react and learn from their ordeal. This, as I have stated,
is more important than catastrophe or death, who wins or loses, who's
in or who's out. Nothing, as Kent notes, "almost sees miracles / But
misery." (*Lear* 2.2.161–62) And the role of misery in human life—
how one masters the art of known and feeling sorrows—is perhaps
what a "tough world" (*Lear* 5.3.315) is mainly about. Selfish passion—such as jealousy in Othello, lust in Antony, revenge in Titus
and Hamlet, hatred and pride in Coriolanus—gives the plays much
of their dynamics. But the deeper feelings come when sorrow is
known and felt and perhaps leads to pity.

The miracle of human betterment and love through suffering is one
of life's major paradoxes, and has been found in all literatures and
philosophies. From Ecclesiastes 7:3–4 comes the most famous statement of that paradox and perhaps the one that must give us the most
hope for triumph in a Hamlet: "Sorrow is better than laughter: for
by the sadness of the countenance the heart is made better. The heart
of the wise is in the house of mourning; but the heart of fools is in
the house of mirth." Whether the heart is indeed made better, or in
some cases is worsened, is a major question in Shakespeare and helps
to define, perhaps better than what we have said about stature and
passion, the true nature of the individual. But the preacher is not
alone in his neatly balanced apothegm. In one of the most popular
books of *consolatio* known to the Renaissance, Boethius writes similarly:

Good fortune byndeth with the beautye of her goodes the hartes or
thoughtes of them that hath them. Evyll fortune unbyndeth mens hartes and
thoughtes by knowledge of her frayle felicitie. And thou seist good fortune
prodigall and not knowing herselfe. Evyl fortune is sober meke and wise, by
exercise of her adversitie.[11]

Cardinal Wolsey's self-discovery, "I feel my heart new opened," may
owe something to Boethius. Wolsey, in Shakespeare, had before his
fall a high-blown pride and ambition. "I know myself now" (*H8*
3.2.377). His advice to Cranmer is "Love thyself last" (3.2.443). Another of the classic lines about sorrow and the heart is spoken by
Virgil's Aeneas, a humane, rather than, like Achilles, a wrathful
hero. The portion most often quoted is "sunt lacrimae rerum," a ne-

cessity for any Shakespearean hero who would feel the full range of sorrow. Here, in translation, is the complete sentence: "Lo Priam! Here, too, virtue has its due rewards; here, too, there are tears for misfortune and mortal sorrows touch the heart."[12] St. Augustine, following Cicero's *Tusculan Disputations,* writes in *The City of God:* "For to lack a sense of sorrow in this mortal life (as a great scholar held) never befalls a man without great stupidity of body and barbarism of mind."[13] (The "great scholar" was Crantor, an Academic philosopher). Augustine in the larger context is pleading for tears through "our human infirmity." And Cicero argued that "we are but sprung from rock but our souls have a strain of tenderness and sensitiveness of a kind to be shaken by distress as by a storm."[14]

The Stoics, to be sure, tended to deplore excessive feeling, even for others. But they were strongly countered by spokesmen for humanity and the heart. A typical argument against them is by M. J. Abernethy in *A Christian and Heavenly Treatise:* "The Stoical *Apathie* (in setting a presse on the heart, exempting the same from all griefe) is a false and phantasticall cure of impatiency."[15] In *Julius Caesar* we shall see how Shakespeare makes dramatically moving Brutus's struggle between the stern philosophy and his fundamentally sensitive heart.

A major benefit of felt sorrow is what we have noted Joseph Conrad saying, that it makes us see in a feeling sense. Donne, who could speak as both feeling poet and eloquent theologian, preached that "as the body of man is mellowed in the grave, but made fit for glory at the resurrection, so the minde of man by suffering is supplied; Adam is made Enosh; and he may see."[16]

Apart from *Lear,* Shakespeare has expressed the impact of pain on feeling most clearly in Duke Senior's speech in *As You Like It.* Here in the forest, he observes, he and his exiled companions benefit rather than suffer from "the icy fang / And churlish chiding of the winter's wind" (2.1.6–7). When he shrinks with cold, he says:

> "This is no flattery." These are counsellors
> That feelingly persuade me what I am.
> Sweet are the uses of adversity,
> Which, like the toad, ugly and venomous,
> Wears yet a precious jewel in his head;
> And this our life, exempt from public haunt,
> Finds tongues in trees, books in the running brook,
> Sermons in stones, and good in everything.
> (2.1.10–17)

Amiens comments: "I would not change it. Happy is your Grace / That can translate the stubbornness of fortune / Into so quiet and so sweet a style" (2.1.18–20). In his comment, Amiens points to the "translation" as almost a standard genre, as in part we have seen that it is.

Another and very important hint of a genre in the Duke's speech is the "Sermons in stones." The image or text of the hard-hearted stone was common in sermons, which, much more homiletic than Shakespeare could be, sought again and again to soften men's hearts. Edward Topsell, in *Times Lamentation,* refers with some impatience to the stolid congregations: "Oh, how stubborn is the conceite of our hard harts, which will not be taught till they smart."[17] And Donne is equally troubled:

That temporall affliction should produce spirituall stoniness and obduration, is innatural, yet ordinary. Therefore doth God propose it, as one of those greatest blessings, which he multiplies upon his people, *I will take away your stony hearts, and give You hearts of flesh.*

He concludes with a terrible warning: "for this petrefaction of the heart, this stupefaction of a man, is the last blow of Gods hand upon the heart of man in this world" (*Sermons* 7:55).

Most modern critics and audiences are skeptical of a religious Shakespeare. And, while agreeing in large part with them, I feel obliged to recognize evidence about the hard heart as it appears in the text. Here we shall observe only a sampling of the critical moments in man's struggle against this stoniness of feelings. We should, in viewing these, notice that they are central and tend to be a dramatic struggle. Claudius's most moving scene is his attempt to pray: "Help, angels! Make assay! / Bow, stubborn knees, and, heart with strings of steel, / Be soft as sinews of the new-born babe!" (*Ham* 3.3.69–71). We like him better for this effort, and our intuition is given strong theological support—partly because it comes from one of the age's most magnetic preachers, William Perkins: "If it be alleged, that every one cannot reach to this beginning of repentance, thus to sorrow for his sinne; then I adde further; if the partie be grieved for the hardness of his heart, whereby it comes to passe, that he cannot grieve, he hath undoubtedly received some portion of godly sorrow."[18] Enobarbus, who has prided himself upon his hardness, is more successful than Claudius, for he dies, as he here intimates, of a broken heart:

> Throw my heart
> Against the flint and hardness of my fault;
> Which, being dried with grief, will break to powder
> And banish all foul thoughts.
>
> (AC 4.9.15–18)

Finally, the most serious crisis of Othello, which will be examined in the text, is his discovery that "my heart is turn'd to stone: I strike it, and it hurts my hand" (*Oth* 4.1.179–80).

Elizabethans had still another avenue toward known and feeling sorrow, and in this path they were tormented, yet blessed, in a way that even the most skeptical of moderns must respect; for much of it has the secular power of the psychological unconsciousness and irrational. I refer to the conscience, the subject of numerous books, notably by the most learned of authorities, William Perkins. Ephraim Huit, however, best anticipated the modern view of conscience: "other faculties may rest," he notes in one of his discussions of dreams; "an obscene dream by night shall not escape its record."[19] Another minister, Gervase Babington, tells typically of this most important aspect of the conscience. Like our first parents, we are unaware, without conscience, of sin. "This of all other is the dreadfullest of blindness, not to see sinne, and this opening of eyes by a piercing blow into my conscience, is consequently most fearfull."[20] A "seared conscience" is the equivalent of the hardened heart, and even King James wrote admonishingly of it. A minister (Jeremiah Dyke), however, presents the most thunderous threat against this moral deadness. Though people "were past feeling in the committing of crime, yet they shall be all feeling in suffering their consciences, and will pare them to the quicke, that they shall feele and most sensibly feel that which here they would not feele."[21]

But enough of what one Shakespearean critic, writing of religious interpretation, calls "a bitter pill to swallow." One can only hope that he will reread plays like *Hamlet, Othello,* and *Macbeth* after ingesting many such pills. Nevertheless, even the most profane of pill-purged critics deserves some easier explanation of what Shakespeare does with felt sorrow. Part of this volume will have more to say about this religious interpretation (though not about sermons!); but for a clearer and simpler explanation than that painfully and imperfectly found in the tragedies, we might look at two romances. These are in many ways tragedies, and their victory over calamity is a clue to what might, in a less easily acceptable genre, be both calamity and some kind of redemption through sorrow.

In *The Winter's Tale,* Leontes becomes an almost insanely jealous
tyrant and is responsible for the death of his young son and the apparent death of his innocent wife (Hermione) and his infant daughter.
His recovery from his fury is quick, but he must spend fifteen years
of sorrow in penance. Learning of his mistake, he orders his court,
"Come and lead me / to these sorrows" (3.2.240–41). Passion is spent
and a heartfelt sorrow must guide him. Paulina, his wife's lady, is his
stern guide. When she sees his true repentance, she would give him,
midway in his ordeal, some relief: "he is touch'd / To the noble heart.
What's gone and what's past help / Should be past grief" (3.2.222–
24). But he is resolute in penance. Near the end of his pilgrimage, a
friend urges him: "Sir, you have done enough, and have perform'd / A
saint-like sorrow. No fault could you make / Which you have not re-
deem'd" (5.1.1–3). And his exiled lord Camillo longs to return to
him after fifteen years' absence, "to whose feeling sorrows I might be
some allay" (4.2.7–8). In the denouement, Leontes is shown what
purports to be the statue of his dead wife, now strangely wrinkled.
Paulina, who has engineered this scheme, points out that the statue is
how Hermione would look if she lived now. He achieves full spiritual
recognition through sorrow:

> As now she might have done,
> So much to my good comfort as it is
> Now piercing to my soul. O, thus she stood,
> Even with such life of majesty, warm life,
> As now it coldly stands, when first I woo'd her!
> I am asham'd; does not the stone rebuke me
> For being more stone than it?
>
> (5.3.32–38)

This recognition is more important than the tragicomic recognition—
somehow less powerful than pure tragedy—that the statue is truly
alive.

In *The Tempest,* we are liable to mistake Prospero as a serene old
man, ideally bringing up his daughter Miranda on a desert island. He
does, indeed, show passion only on about three occasions. With the
help of his spirit Ariel, he is engaged in finding an ideal mate for his
daughter and in providing penance for his brother and the others who
had exiled and wronged him. He could be merely a severe, insensitive
minister of justice, contrasting with the animal-like passionate Cali-
ban and his own marveling daughter Miranda. She, near the very be-

ginning of the action, shows to advantage by her grief at the apparent loss at sea that her father has coldly devised by his magic:

> O, I have suffer'd
> With those that I saw suffer. A brave vessel,
> Who had, no doubt, some noble creature in her,
> Dash'd all to pieces! O, the cry did knock
> Against my very heart.
>
> (1.2.5–9)

But Prospero reassures her that no damage has resulted from "The direful spectacle of the wrack, which touch'd / The very virtue of compassion in thee" (1.2.26–27). Prospero is, actually, a mage with moral feeling. He has Ariel, disguised as a Harpy, prophesy to the villains and scoundrels, who have been in agony during their shipwreck, that "Ling'ring perdition, worse than any death / Can be at once, shall step by step attend / You and your ways" (3.3.77–79). What shall follow "is nothing but heart's sorrow / And a clear life ensuing" (3.3.81–82). At their "heart's sorrow," even the amoral Ariel is almost moral. His affection would be moved "were I human" (5.1.20). Prospero then makes manifest that he has not been a man of stone.

He too has endured passion, but in the speech that sums up one major idea of the play, he says he "relishes all as sharply passion as they" (5.1.23–24), for he is one of "their kind"—that is, a man. But his "nobler reason" conquers his "fury" (5.1.23,24), and he realizes that "The rarer action is / In virtue than in vengeance" (5.1.27–28).

We may, without too firm a generalization, infer that sorrow can be "worse than any death" (3.3.77). Equally important, we gain a crucial insight into the responsibility that humanity has when, though "struck to the quick" (5.1.25), it must act with a feeling and a reasonableness above passion. This insight leads us to what some Elizabethans (and many of us today) might have felt to be the most urgent concern of resolution in Shakespeare's tragedies: that humanity not lose its most valued qualities.

Threatened Humanity

This introduction has proposed and means to test the hypothesis that one of the most anxious and dramatic concerns in the tragedies is not whether a hero dies or fails materially. Rather it is in Augustine's maxim that what matters is *how* he suffers. Many Elizabethans, well instructed to be sure, would argue that the survival and meaning of humanity are dependent upon man's "capability and godlike reason" (*Ham* 4.4.38)—and that these characteristics, rather than passive or heroic traits, make him a man. Theodore Spencer, in *Shakespeare and the Nature of Man,* has written ably on the conflicting attitudes toward man in the age and in Shakespeare: the optimistic and the pessimistic views. His important thesis is that the conflict of these views made then what we cannot have now: tragedy. It is therefore unnecessary here to go through this material, now fortunately accessible and respected.

The major threat to humanity, however, is macrocosmic. If man, the microcosm, moves from an ordered nature (usually in disobeying what Ulysses in *Troilus and Cressida* calls "the specialty of rule,"1.3.78), if rude appetite rather than reason prevails, not only man but also the macrocosm will undergo frightful upheaval. Next to Ulysses', the most famous and eloquent statement of this inevitable consequence is Richard Hooker's in *Of the Laws of Ecclesiastical Polity* (The First Book). There he darkly predicts that "if nature should intermit her course, and leave altogether though it were but for a while the observation of her own laws . . ., what would become of man himself, whom these things now do serve? See we not plainly that obedience of creatures unto the law of nature is the stay of the whole world?"[22] Though less famous and moving, Sir Thomas Elyot's *The Governor* (1531) puts it more succinctly and with specific blame upon man for his own descent into chaos:

> More over take away ordre from all thyngs what should remayne? Certes nothinge finally, except some man wolde imagine eftsone *chaos:* which of some is expounde a confuse mixture. Also where there is any lacke of ordre needes must be perpetuell conflicte: in thynges subject to Nature nothynge of hym selfe onely may be nourished: but when he hath distroyed that where he doth participate by the ordre of his creation, he hym selfe of necessitie must there perisshe, whereof ensueth universal dissolution.[23]

The passage gives valuable context to Othello's premonition about what would happen if his severely ordered life should be shaken by the loss of Desdemona: "Perdition catch my soul / But I do love thee! And when I love thee not / Chaos is come again" (*Oth* 3.3.90–92). So important was the anxiously held, and precarious, humanity of civilization in England, that a long warning about a possible dissolution occurs in the government mandated *Homilies*, one of which was required to be read each Sunday. A portion of the homily entitled "An Exhortacion Concerning Good Order and Obedience to Rulers and Magistrate" (1547) warns: "For where there is no right ordre there reigneth all abuse, carnell liberty, enormitie, syn, and babilonicall confusion."[24] Evil, in the era and often in Shakespeare, is not petty or purely personal. Gratuitious evil does occur mysteriously. But more often there is a larger breakdown lifting into lofty suffering and tragedy all kinds of inhuman dissension. Even as early in Shakespeare's career as the long, tragic narrative poem *The Rape of Lucrece*, there is a characteristic picture of frail humanity in the world of beasts and lawlessness. Lucrece, a virtuous matron, pleads for her honor against the lustful Tarquin about to ravage her. Shakespeare's narrator describes here the plight of later humanity in the dramatic tragedies:

> Here with a cockatrice's dead-killing eye
> He rouseth up himself and makes a pause:
> While she, the picture of pure pietie,
> Like a white hind under the gripe's sharp claws,
> Pleads in a wilderness where are no laws,
> To the rough beast that knows no gentle right
> Nor ought but his foul appetite.
>
> (540–46)

Man in a world of beasts, without laws and hence with obvious barbarism, is the subject of Shakespeare's first tragedy, *Titus Andronicus*. But the most powerful outcry of foreboding uttered by a feeling and civilized humanity is found in *King Lear*. The virtuous Albany is horrified and prophetically almost right in his plea for the aged Lear in a bestial world "where are no laws." Albany addresses Lear's heartless daughters:

> What have you done?
> Tigers, not daughters, what have you perform'd?
> A father, and a gracious aged man,
> Whose reverence even the head-lugg'd bear would lick,
> Most barbarous, most degenerate! have you madded.
> Could my good brother suffer you to do it?
> A man, a prince, by him so benefited!
> If that the heavens do not their visible spirits
> Send quick down to tame these vile offences
> It will come.

> Humanity must perforce prey upon itself.
> Like monsters of the deep.
>
>   (4.2.39–50)

The mighty misanthropic curses of Timon, a man turning beast, portend the dissolution of humanity.

Albany's warning stresses the near sanctity of man and his contrast with a beast. Manliness in Shakespeare usually means courage and is an important aspect of tragedy. But *man* connotes the gentle, feeling virtues that protect humanity from barbarism. *Macbeth* stresses this connotation. The thane's "fiend-like" wife (5.8.69), in meditating an ambitious murder, is worried by the gentle manliness of her husband: "Yet do I fear thy nature; / It is too full o' th' milk of human kindness / To catch the nearest way" (1.5.14–16).

In fact, much of the tension of the play will result from his losing this human kindness (which might easily be read *humankindness*). For instance, just before his Lady accuses him of having relinquished his promised manliness ("then you were a man," 1.7.49), the two meanings of the term become importantly contrasted in self-justification: "I dare do all that may become a man; Who dares do more is none" (1.7.46–47). Macduff also stresses the better meaning of the word in his exchange later with Malcolm. When Malcolm tells him a possible remedy to allay his grief over his family's slaughter, "Dispute it like a man," Macduff gives way to human grief: "I shall do so; / But I must feel it as a man" (4.3.220–221).

Mankind, then, can be threatened by a dangerous disorder, which in the greatest plays is lifted to macrocosmic proportion. More frequently, it is threatened, in a way that fells Macbeth, by a narrowing humanity. "Tragic man,"[25] to use Richard Sewell's phrase, must assuredly have those traits that according to A. P. Rossiter give him the essential stature, "passional distinction."[26] But the passion, especially since it comes from self-love, can diminish him as a rational creature, and usually can conduce to his tragedy. Even a grandly passionate man, if we are to respond in a manner worthy of high tragedy, must not be, in Hamlet's words, "a beast, no more" (4.4.35). But the problem is by no means so simple as reason versus passion. Nor should we narrowly compare, for example, the passion of an Antony with that of a Romeo.

We will approach infinitely various characters and their various agonies and sometimes greater triumphs with open minds. Not impossibly, the most important enduring response—one that will sustain us in our lesser ordeals—is suggested in Duke Senior's observation:

> Thou seest we are not all alone unhappy.
> This wide and universal theatre
> Presents more woeful pageants than the scene
> Wherein we play in.
>
> *(AYL,* 2.7.136–39)

And perhaps this is not too far from Wolsey's "I feel my heart new opened."

Chapter Two
Titus Andronicus
Imperfect but Strong Beginnings

More analyzed than read, performed, or studied, Shakespeare's first tragedy deserves to be better known if not loved. It is clearly the work of a master, despite its excessive violence—a violence not controlled by the powerful, less ornate poetry of the later plays. Shakespeare was not, as has been suspected, seeking almost cosmic, laughable outrage. As with his dedicated early tragic narrative poem *The Rape of Lucrece* (also involving a rape), he was soberly trying his best; and even an early best for him was superior to what was being done by any of his contemporaries. True, he was possibly taking advantage of the sweepingly popular appeal of Thomas Kyd's *The Spanish Tragedy* and other dramas of crude revenge, and perhaps the Senecan *Thyestes,* which has similar cannibalism. But he followed Ovid, too, in a tale of Philomel and her rape and mutilation from *Metamorphoses.* And in this narrative poem he possibly found the theme, as Eugene Waith has suggested, of men changing into beasts, as well as a style that makes carnage less revolting.[1]

Also, the beginning artist in tragedy seems to have worked naturally and seriously among the popular Elizabethan designs for the tragedy of blood. For he was, though improvising and experimenting, always aware of his audience and fellow dramatists. More important, he was impelled, with what seems to have been a mixture of studious structure and his conscious anticipation, to use an amazing number of tragic techniques, themes, and characters that inform his later plays. There is a moderately imposing, though old and feeble, general as protagonist, a general who has prospered more in war than, upon his return to the craftily politic of Rome, he will in peace. These totally depraved characters include the stupidly evil Emperor Saturninus, the lustful Tamora, Queen of the Goths, and the devil incarnate Aaron. There is also a dramatic relationship of which he never tired, that between father (Titus) and daughter, the almost physically dehumanized Lavinia. Titus not only has moderate stature but also he has what must be considered a passion: a sense of pride that compels him to kill his son Mutius who tries to prevent an enforced marriage between Lavinia and the new emperor, the evil, but not interestingly so, Saturninus.

Tragic Grounds

It is not only his passionate stature that brings about the suffering of Titus and his family. As almost invariably, the hero's tragedy is a mixture of a flawed character and an evil that is not always clearly an extension of his inmost nature.

Titus, several critics (notably Irving Ribner) have argued, is justly tormented because he not only kills his son in prideful passion but also presides over sacrificial mutilation of Alarbus, the eldest son of Tamora. But there is not a comforting sense of deserved tragedy, despite his inhumanity in the later Thyestian feast in which, in artful revenge, he is cook and serves up "pasties" (5.3.189) to Tamora, consisting of the mutilated bodies of her two sons, Chiron and Demetrius. For the most part, he is shown as a patriot and as loving parent and brother. And his tragic mistake could more likely, as he later thinks, be that he loyally nominates what to Elizabethans would be the rightful heir, Saturninus, instead of the virtuous but junior brother Bassianus as emperor. He also, in what is an issue in revenge tragedy (including *The Spanish Tragedy, Hamlet,* and *Othello*), suffers in an attempt to achieve justice before revenge. And he turns to revenge only when his "miseries are more than may be borne" (3.1.243). These miseries include seeing and caring for his daughter, who enters (in one of the most demanding stage directions ever written) with "her hands cut off, and her tongue cut out, and ravaged" (2.4). They include sacrificing his arm in a gruesomely sadistic trick by Aaron, who assures him that two of his sons' lives will be spared if he sends the emperor his arm. In exchange for his arm, which had fought for Rome, he is presented, along with the severed arm, the heads of his sons. In one of the better dramatic touches in this tale of unrelieved gloom, Titus merely responds with a "Ha, ha, ha!" (3.1.264). The theme does indeed threaten to be absurd, showing man at the brink of meaningless torment. But Titus also asks with the sort of heartrending questioning that will be in later tragedies, "When will this fearful slumber have an end?" (3.1.252). It is a kind of nightmare world in which the qualities of mankind and the gods

are dimly conceived and their worth questioned—not logically, as in
Hamlet, but in a dream.

Titus, moreover, as we shall more fully see, improves in some re-
spects, even under inhuman ordeals. He fully accepts, as his son
Lucius can scarcely do, the grotesquely metamorphosed Lavinia as his
daughter. Even the compassionate Marcus had presented her as "This
was your daughter" (3.1.63). Titus exclaims that she still is. Stand-
ing, despite intimations of madness,

> as one upon a rock
> Environed with a wilderness of sea,
> Who marks the waxing tide grow wave by wave,
> Expecting even when some envious surge
> Will in his brinish bowels swallow him,

he turns lovingly to his child:

> But that which gives my soul the greatest spurn
> Is dear Lavinia, dearer than my soul.
> Had I but seen thy picture in this plight,
> It would have madded me: what shall I do
> Now I behold thy lively body so?
>
> (3.1.94–105)

The verse lacks the broken passionate rhythms of Shakespeare's later
tragedies, but there is an earnest of deeply powerful feeling in his
lines, some proof that Shakespeare meant our heart to be with Titus.

Equally important, Titus's inflexible pride is replaced by pity and
an ability to see others feelingly. He is a remarkably early hint of Lear
in becoming involved in humanity, and in his almost incredible ability, for a stern Roman warrior, to weep.

Even in the midst of a "meaningless" sorrow, when feeling for human beings seems almost impossible, when he can complain that
there was no reason for these miseries (3.1.219), Titus is moved by
the killing of a fly. True, like so many of his later actions, this one
has an element of irrationality hardly distinguishable from madness (a
revenge play staple), and true that the pity is quickly converted to
hate when his brother says that the fly is really a metamorphosis of
Aaron. But this curious episode—something that Hereward Price
would call a "mirror scene" because it stops the plot and reflects upon
character or theme[2]—shows that Titus is still humanly moved. When

Marcus bizarrely strikes at a fly with his knife, Titus cannot endure
the spectacle:

> Out on thee, murderer! Thou kill'st my heart;
> Mine eyes are cloyed with view of tyranny.
> A deed of death done on the innocent
> Becomes not Titus' brother. Get thee gone.
>   (3.2.54–57)

When Marcus protests that he has "but killed a fly" (3.2.59), Titus
shows his sense of family tragedy, though the language has a pretty
rather than a powerful accent unluckily typical of even the most painful passion in the play:

> "But"? How if that fly had a father and a mother?
> How would he hang his slender gilded wings
> And buzz lamenting doings in the air!
> Poor harmless fly,
> That with his pretty buzzing melody
> Came here to make us merry, and thou hast killed him.
>   (3.2.60–65)

Titus, then, despite his crazed revenge, does progress from a man
of rigorous honor to a man who can feel. Is he in any formal way
deserving of the terrible "punishment" that changes him? Probably
not. But since this is the case in most Shakespeare's tragedies, we
must become aware of an almost invariable ingredient that Shakespeare employs to prevent his heroes from becoming inhuman pawns
of fate or external evil. This is the extremely human ingredient of
moral choice. Shakespeare gives Titus a climactic moment of decision.
And thereby, human character is at least partially affirmed. By act 3
Titus has "not another tear to shed" (3.1.266). Also, his tears would
blind him from finding "Revenge's cave" (3.1.270). He has the few
remaining Andronici encircle him, "That I may turn me to each one
of you, / And swear unto my soul to right your wrongs. / The vow is
made" (3.1.277–79). An almost sacred vow usually will mark the
peripety of a Shakespearean tragedy. It is a commitment in soul, irre-
versible, made with ritual. It is peculiarly appropriate for this tragedy, which, almost choreographed, has so much formal kneeling.
But, unlike the situation in other plays, it does not quite succeed in
hardening the hero's heart.

A Wilderness of Tigers

Perhaps an audience's response is the best clue to how blame in the play is to be assigned. And this response is almost irresistibly conditioned not by the way the Andronici behave but by the environment in which they live. This environment is called by Titus "a wilderness of tigers" (3.1.55), and his explanation for the evils is simply that "Tigers must prey, and Rome affords no prey / But me and mine" (3.1.56–57). It is perhaps a major defect in the play that, more than in any other of Shakespeare's tragedies, evil is pervasive, extreme, and usually gratuitous. Though bestiality motivates much of the evil, even the concept of tigers perforcedly preying is too easy a reason for the quasi-human tortures that spread throughout the action. Audiences, often to their sense of shame, find themselves not uplifted by their emotions. Instead they later recognize that they have indulged in an orgy of hatred and that even the utmost of barbaric punishment is inadequate for their appetite. It is not quite enough that Aaron should be set "breast-deep in earth" (5.3.179) or, more appropriately, that Tamora should be thrown "to beasts and birds to prey," for "her life was beastly and devoid of pity" (5.3.198–99). Probably an audience with a typical sense of humanity is both relieved and repelled by the denouement. If the audience blames Titus, it must in large part blame itself. But exposure of hidden anger is not psychologically wasted, and, as usual, Shakespeare has not seriously erred.

The "tigers" are some of the most loathsome specimens of humanity that an Elizabethan could create or countenance. Moving insidiously or brutally among the somber Andronici, they are generally devoid of moral feeling and have, except for the emperor, a ghoulish sense of humor. They have, especially Aaron, a quality of sport and glee in their monstrosities. Marcus expresses well the unique kind of treatment suffering receives in the play: "To weep with them that weep doth ease some deal; / But sorrow flouted at is double death" (3.1.244–45). This view is theatrically significant, too, in that the response of an onstage audience (the other characters) can console or disturb the outer audience.

Demetrius and Chiron make almost unbearable, though not without some sense of sick humor, the spectacle of Lavinia whom they have stripped of loveliness and womanliness. Instead of graceful arms she has, they rejoice gleefully, "stumps" (2.4.4). (Aaron's phrase is even more heartlessly apt: they have "trimmed her," 5.1.93). Aaron and Tamora laugh almost uncontrollably at the trick played with Titus's arm. Of the lustful brothers and of Aaron's reaction to the deed, a messenger says, "thy grief their sports" (3.1.288).

Of all the moral degenerates, however, Aaron is the most fascinating and primal. He is black, lustful, and curly haired, features that were attributed to Blackamoors. But Shakespeare does not limit his evil to his racial origin. Although accompanying Tamora, he seems to come unneeded, from nowhere. Differing from villains in greater plays, he bears no relevance to the good characters, for his evil is not an allegorized or metamorphosed form of some tendency innate in them. He teaches us no lesson about the precariousness of true humanity. He is only meaninglessly evil. Tamora may have just grievance against Titus; Aaron has none. And yet he is perhaps the most vital character in the play. His relation of his sickening crime has zest. It is almost welcome in a somber, lachrymose play in which evil is merely lamented. Aaron makes evil a more interestingly specific commentary on human misery. It is going only a little too far to call it comic relief. What is more, his lust for Tamora leads to the fine antic scenes in which he almost humanly defends the coal-black son whom he has fathered by her. The nurse in shame and fear brings the illegitimate baby to Tamora's son for disposal. To Demetrius's proposed solution, "I'll broach the tadpole on my rapier's point" (4.2.85), Aaron rises to nearly human, almost heroic passion: "He dies upon my scimitar's sharp point / That touches my first-born son and heir" (4.2.91–92). And there is no cringing, but brave wit, in his question to Demetrius, "Stay, murderous villain, will you kill your brother?" (4.2.87). He plans to conceal the "black slave" who "smiles upon the father" (4.2.120) by disposing of possible witnesses. His stabbing of the nurse is, out of context, simply loathsome; but his grotesque humor has vigor. He mocks her death cry by "Weke, weke! / So cries a pig prepared to the spit." (4.2.146–47). This action, to be sure, is execrable and reduces humanity almost to its lowest point. But his final defense of his son has some manliness. And though we are not moved by his loyalty, we prefer him to the stupid, lustful louts—sons of Tamora. Of the active evil in the play, we can only say that it is not cosmic, but merely distastefully ugly and unintelligent. Aaron gives it its only life.

Telling Sorrows to the Stones

But tragedies depending for their meaning on villains tend not to be Shakepeare's most profound study in threatened humanity or in the disturbing alienation between man and the gods. There is a more frighteningly intractable sort of affliction—given a remarkably early prominence in *Titus Andronicus*—in which environment is unresponsive to human pleas for justice or pity. Aaron describes ably a part of this "wilderness of tigers" in which the outrages occur. He advises Demetrius and Chiron:

> The woods are ruthless, dreadful, deaf, and dull.
> There speak and strike, brave boys, and take your turns,
> There serve your lust, shadowed from heaven's eye,
> And revel in Lavinia's treasury.
>
> (2.1.128–31)

If there is any philosophical theme in the play, suggesting the plight and hopelessness of humanity, it is a constant, futile pleading to the "ruthless, dreadful, deaf, and dull"—probably even without the "heaven's eye" that Aaron mentions. But the improvement in the good, but flawed Titus is significantly due to his change from a hard, though not evil, judge and warrior to a man who learns much about man's needs because his own have made him plead not only for himself but mainly for others. We thereby undergo one of the repeated miracles of Shakespeare's tragedies: we grow to like, even love, a man who begins so unpromisingly without feeling.

Titus's first rejection of a plea is that of the anguished Tamora that he will not sacrifice her first-born son, Alarbus. She may not have been an innately cruel woman, although later we learn that much of her murderous anger against Titus is that she has had to kneel on the city streets. Although obdurate, Titus may be acting through religious compulsion to perform an execution-ritual that will let his slain sons rest. But there is no such excuse—only passionate honor—in his rejecting for a long scene of pleading his kneeling sons' petition that they be permitted to bury the brother Mutius who in a rightful cause had tried to save Lavinia from marriage to Saturninus. Lavinia herself is the next to plead that Demetrius and Chiron will spare her virtue. She urges the sons to beseech the mother, who must know womanly feelings. But these are "tiger's young" (2.3.142), and Demetrius tells Tamora to ignore Lavinia's tears: "be your heart to them / as unrelenting flint to drops of rain" (2.3.140–41). Upon Tamora's brutal rejection, Lavinia links lack of feminine feeling with beastliness as she cries, "No grace? No womanhood? Ah beastly creature, / The blot and enemy to our general name!" (2.3.182–83).

Then comes the all-important necessity for Titus himself to plead. This necessity, and its enactment, are given a progression that will not be forgotten in *King Lear* by making the hero pathetically old and understandably set in his ways. Titus's ordeal begins when his sons are to be executed for supposedly killing the emperor's brother Bassianus and throwing him into a pit. Actually, the villains are the empress's sons, but Titus doesn't know this, and his first blow is to his honor. He shows, nevertheless, for the first time, love and compassion by falling on his "feeble knee" (2.3.288) and begging for his sons' life "with tears not lightly shed" (2.3.289). He had heretofore not wept for "two and twenty sons" because they died in honor's lofty bed (3.1.9–10).

The agony is the greater because, a proud man, he had never begged, never had to depend on "the aged wrinkles in [his] cheeks" (3.1.7), never had to bend from his dignity to a groveling, almost clownish demeanor. Lying on the ground, he gets no response. Lucius tells him that "no tribune hears you speak" (3.1.32). But plead he must, and "Therefore I tell my sorrows to the stones" (3.1.37). The verse of pleading becomes more passionate and moving than before, even as Titus becomes, temporarily at least, a warmer man.

Upon the gruesome response to his prayer, when his sons' heads and his own hand are brought to him, he raises his one remaining hand to the heavens. And in a later episode he and his daughter present an almost blasphemous spectacle of hapless man as they both lift their stumps to the apparently absent gods. For this is the ultimate challenge to pleading in the play:

> O, here I lift this one hand up to heaven,
> And bow this feeble ruin to the earth.
> If any power pities wretched tears,
> To that I call.
>
> (3.1.206–9)

And he asks Lavinia to do the like. It is Marcus, the one flawless and compassionate male character in the play—one who must speak chorically—who makes the great and unanswered challenge: "O heavens, can you hear a good man groan / And not relent, or not compassion him?" (4.1.123–24). But even Marcus is not able to suppress perhaps the most blasphemous suggestion made by a character (other than Gloucester) in Shakespeare: "O, why should nature build so foul a den, / Unless the gods delight in tragedies?" (4.1.59–60).

Resolution

There is no conclusive answer to the most significant questions in Shakespeare. In his sonnet "Shakespeare," Matthew Arnold has made one of the most important pronouncements about the poet: "Others abide our question. Thou art free. / We ask and ask—Thou smilest and art still, / Out-topping knowledge."[3] Particularly in this rough-hewn play there is no moral or philosophical answer to our question, or to Titus's or Marcus's. Yet almost none of Shakespeare's tragedies, even this one, is without some kind of resolution—sometimes an exultation—making it more than a chaotic, depressing ending. Here, as noticed, we are passionately, but not morally, satisfied by the unparalleled revenge on the villains. More in the Shakespearean manner is the union of the few remaining virtuous people at the ending. Ritually, they come to the fallen Titus, kneel, and kiss him. And the populace is sympathetic and at one, even accepting the conquering return of Titus's son Lucius at the head of a Gothic army. Most typically Shakespearean of all, the union comes in the state, and almost in the last line. It is, in the best sense, a political resolution. Lucius, now emperor, disposes bestially of the beasts before pronouncing, as his last words: "Then, afterwards, to order so the state, / That like events may ne'er it ruinate "(5.3.203–4). Family and state, though reduced, have survived. "Like events" will have like ordering—humanly sacrificed but not fatally reductive—in the greatest of Shakespeare's tragedies.

Chapter Three
Romeo and Juliet

Death-Marked Love

Romeo and Juliet differs in one important respect from the other tragedies. Although it is marked by intense passion and although its tragic course is at least in part due to the most irresistible of all emotions, love, the two protagonists are not of the tragic stature found in the other plays. Romeo, it is true, kills, besides himself, two other men, and Juliet kills herself. But neither is imposingly built on a large scale, and they are, perforce, more passive than active. They are the victims of what the opening Chorus calls "piteous overthrows" (*RJ* Prol. 7). So we can feel pity, but not terror, at their fates.

This is not to say that the play is inferior to or less moving than the others. It is perfect in its kind. It shows pure, youthful, tragic love in a poetry consummately suited to that love. The pity is poignant enough to evoke tears, as it often does, in an audience. And the characters, though less complex as well as less grand than those that Shakespeare would create in his maturity, are perfect for their roles and perhaps more compellingly lovable than almost any others. They are far younger than any other of Shakespeare's protagonists. Juliet is thirteen and Romeo still young enough to have tearful tantrums and other uncontrolled emotions. Most important in assessing both the quality and the tragic effect of the play is the fact that it belongs to one of the most dependably heartrending of genres in all of world literature: *Liebestod,* or love-death. Well-known examples are Hero and Leander and Tristam and Iseult, while Antony and Cleopatra, as Shakespeare conceived them, are grander in their passion but not at all pitiable. The "death-marked" couple, as Shakespeare describes them in the opening Chorus, should be young and innocent— in all senses. They are not so much agents as hapless victims; and they are as sexually inexperienced as Antony and Cleopatra are richly experienced, and hence have the idealistic ardor of first true love. Juliet, indeed, is so artless that she proposes marriage to Romeo.

Romeo, to be sure, is less cloistered and hence less artless than his loved one. He "consorts" (3.1.45) the streets of Verona in the company of "lusty" (1.2.26) gallants, notably Mercutio and Benvolio. But these two look upon love as a sport to be taken wittily and even bawdily, even to be viewed as a softening influence on their realistic, sometimes brawling interests. Mercutio, in particular, is skillfully created, not only as a spirited, knowledgeable character, but also as a foil to Romeo's dreamy subjection to love. Mercutio knows all about sex, but he will not let it give him more than sport. His attitude is evident in his indecently lively, often bawdy speech, making him perhaps the most interesting and complex character in the play. When Romeo returns intoxicated by his meeting with Juliet on the balcony, Mercutio jollies him in typical fashion:

Why is this not better than groaning for love? Now art thou sociable, now art thou Romeo; now art thou what thou art, by art as by nature. For this drivelling love is like a great natural [i.e., fool] that runs lolling up and down to hide his bauble in a hole. (2.4.83–87)

Juliet's innocence (uninformed but by no means unintelligent) is similarly emphasized by her contrast with her nurse. This aged woman is not without her human vulnerability. She repeats again and again her loss of her daughter and her husband. But she also has a zestful memory of sex. Her favorite, ultimately tiresome anecdote about her husband is his indecent jest that Juliet, upon maturity, will fall not on her face but on her back. And, when the secretly married Juliet is to be forced to marry Paris, her advice is more than one of realistic acceptance; it is that marriage to Paris will be desirable because the banished Romeo is no longer of use to her. Juliet's superior idealism is made appealing when she turns indignantly on this, her last available confidante.

But though both Mercutio and the nurse are perfect foils to the young couple's pure love, they should not be regarded merely as such. Each has traits that are admirable and especially authentic. In fact, it may be conjectured that Mercutio had to be sacrificed midway in the play because he was threatening to make Romeo appear pallid. At any rate, Shakespeare's professional knowledge of the theater surely instructed him that the audience, given only a cloying duet of "sweet sorrow" (2.2.185), would on its own begin to snicker. By supplying his own comic and realistic elements in the action and speech, Shakespeare controlled the play and the emotions himself.

Star-crossed Lovers

That the lovers are inevitably death-marked is questioned by some critics. Certainly much of the grip the action has on the audience depends upon a constant hope that the couple will be saved and the family hatred allayed. Only a change or two is needed. We must therefore look more closely at the fabric and structure of the play to see whether Shakespeare has indeed made the ominous "star-crossed" (Prol.6) warning of the Chorus organic to the language and action. The Chorus, even though we do not have to accept totally so brief and epigrammatic a summary of a complex play, tells us that the lovers are necessary sacrifices. Nothing but their death can "bury their parents' strife" (Prol.8).

In a play so hauntingly rich in imagery, written for an age sensitive to the foreboding of the stars, the language makes us constantly aware of an ominous outcome. Caroline Spurgeon's study of the iterative imagery[1] shows how Shakespeare pictured, and not merely described, the tragedy. The dominant image is of a dark world only momentarily lighted by flashes of beauty and lightning. Even without relying on imagery, we feel in the lovers' presentiments a star-crossed destiny. Romeo goes to the banquet given by the Capulets only reluctantly. Benvolio had told them that the way to conquer his doting love for Rosaline is to "examine other beauties" (1.1.226). In this he is right, but tragically so, for he is inadvertently a cause of several deaths. The play puts more truth in feelings than in reason. And so when Benvolio berates Romeo for not hurrying to the party, Romeo's intuition is truer than his friend's common sense. He fears that he will come too early,

> For my mind misgives
> Some consequence, yet hanging in the stars,
> Shall bitterly begin his fearful date
> With this night's revels, and expire the term
> Of a despised life closed in my breast,
> By some vile forfeit of untimely death.
> (1.4.106–11)

Juliet, too, accurately feels the ominous threat in what had first been an ecstatic vow of union with Romeo. She tells her almost-betrothed lover when she has known him only an hour or two:

> Although I joy in thee,
> I have no joy of this contract to-night.
> It is too rash, too unadvised, too sudden;
> Too like the lightning, which doth cease to be
> Ere one can say "It lightens."
> (2.2.116–20)

And when the two part after their marriage night, both of them, despite valiant attempts to be hopeful of a reunion, are gripped by a more potent realization. It is more potent even as Shakespeare's dark images are more potent than the reasonableness of daylight. These young impressionistic lovers reach, in their own intuitive way, the misgivings of the rational friar; and it is not venturing too far into a biographical heresy to say that they pictured—though with less perspective—the brevity of their bright light in a dark world in a way not too different from the poet's. At any rate, their premonitions upon separating are not only true in superficial or abstract happening, but also they are poetically accurate in a specific sense. Juliet cries, even as she sees:

> O God, I have an ill-divining soul!
> Methinks I see thee, now thou art so low,
> As one dead in the bottom of a tomb.
> Either my eyesight fails, or thou lookest pale.
> (3.5.54–57)

Romeo is similarly the victim of a true vision: "And trust me, love, in my eye so do you. / Dry sorrow drinks our blood. Adieu, adieu!" (3.5.58–59).

Surely the power and depth of the poetry should dispel any doubt that the lovers are star-crossed. It would be impossible, merely by changing events or unlucky timing, to make this a happy play, although this has been attempted by producers. In the seventeenth century, a "happy" ending was supplied merely by having Juliet awaken from her drugged sleep a few minutes earlier. This version of the play alternated in production with Shakespeare's version. Though foolish, the "improved" version is a tribute to the urgency with which the drama made the audience need reassurance, however inferior event is to theme.

Nevertheless, Shakespeare has also made the structure and events of the play enforce the theme of fate. According to Bertrand Evans,[2] Shakespeare could not make the play a tragedy of fate merely by calling it so (or, one must add, by making fate more expressively pervade the poetry). He had to show how fate worked. Evans's theory is that he did so by making all characters in it unaware of what was happening. All of them had discrepant levels of awareness that led them to fatal errors that they would not, if better informed, have committed. Thus, in the raucous first scene, the feud is introduced by brawling serving men of the rival houses, Montague and Capulet, who fight swaggeringly because "The quarrel is between our masters, and us their men" (1.1.18–19). These self-important simpletons will never learn their fatal role. Then, in rising order of importance, further partisans of each side enter. Tybalt, a grimly humorless version of Mercutio whose one interest is Montague-hunting, enters and starts a duel with Romeo's friend Benvolio. Then the Capulet and Montague fathers join the ruckus. And finally—as always events happen in this play—at exactly the wrong time, the Prince enters and pronounces a warning on both houses. No motive or understanding is evident to anyone in this scene of outrage, or in its origins.

Later in the play occurs the major instance of unawareness: the secret marriage of Romeo and Juliet. No one except the priest who marries them (Friar Laurence) and the nurse knows of the marriage. Most of the ensuing events of mischance and hate might have been avoided if the marriage had been known. Another major misunderstanding is Romeo's mistaken belief that Juliet is actually dead in the Capulet vault. He thinks so because his well-meaning servant Balthazar rides posthaste to Mantua to tell him so. With this "knowledge," Romeo kills himself.

Stony Limits

Evans's theory of unawareness is useful, but perhaps does not go deeply enough below the structure into the theme. Unawareness can take more profound form than ignorance of what is happening. Its deepest meaning in *Romeo and Juliet* is suggested by Romeo's explanation to Juliet of how he got over the Capulet walls to see her: "stony limits cannot hold love out" (2.2.67). The tragic symbol of the play may well be the high, closely guarded walls of the Capulet estate. These keep out not merely romantic love but also the kind of awareness of other people that makes union and human feeling possible. Obdurate separation and stoniness of heart are the major agents of evil in the play. Unlike other tragedies, this play has no human villain. In this respect, it has the potential for a more basic commentary on mankind than those plays in which evil is comfortably attributed to some man or woman who can be blamed and hated.

It is not primarily unawareness of Juliet's clandestine marriage that makes old Capulet storm cruelly at his daughter when she refuses to marry his choice, Paris. Nor, probably, would knowledge of the secret marriage prevent Lady Capulet from her cruel passion for blood revenge on Romeo. Tybalt's murderous hatred of the Montagues is due to no unawareness of what they have done. His is the more general ignorance of the play: a feud-hatred that goes back for generations and that needs for correction a cleansing of evil passions in the soul. Only love can o'erperch the walls of separations.

One of the major problems of the play is why such lovable children as Romeo and Juliet should be central victims in this tragedy of hate. Juliet poignantly expresses her bewilderment and pain at how life has treated her. She has fallen in love with one of the "enemy" family. Shakespeare has masterfully confined the young people's questioning to what we might expect of their age. Juliet cannot understand the necessity for separation. Her "What's in a name?" (2.2.43) is justly, despite its naive sense of discovery, one of the most famous of Shakespeare's questions. Juliet questions, in the terms of piteousness one would expect of a girl, why her mother would force her to marry Paris. The question she cries, which, in more portentous form, will be asked again in *King Lear,* is: "Is there no pity sitting in the clouds / That sees into the bottom of my grief?" (3.5.198–99). And in a similar vein she complains, seeking comfort, alone, from the nurse, a woman hopelessly incapable of communion with her: "Alack, alack, that heaven should practice stratagems / Upon so soft a subject as myself!" (3.5.211–12).

She is left increasingly separate, once Romeo is banished, from all counsel except for the Friar whom she cannot fully trust. Her separation is, indeed, given almost thematic importance by the banishment. *Banished* is the most painful word either lover can hear. It even has theological overtones, as Romeo points out to the Friar, for it is the ultimate punishment, pain of loss *(poena damni),* or separation from God: "O friar, the damned use that word in hell; / Howling attends it!" (3.3.47–48). For Juliet, the separation from Romeo (and her nurse, and her mother, and her father) means that she is cut off during her moment of greatest trial for a child: taking the potion and seeing the images of horror in the Capulet tomb following it. Much is connoted in her resolution: "My dismal scene I needs must act alone" (4.3.19).

Romeo does not question so pathetically as Juliet, but his guiltlessness becomes more apparent as he improves in character from the ordeal. Juliet has not had to improve; but Romeo, at first a whining lover of himself in the role of lover, passionate but not truly reaching out of himself, has much to learn. It is not his fault that he must confront Tybalt. But Shakespeare does not entirely exempt him from the test of moral choice that will make him more than a pitiable victim. When Tybalt returns from having wounded Mercutio, Romeo knows that his friend is now dead. Romeo cannot honorably evade him, but his words of hateful vengeance take the consecrated form of denying heaven and giving up his cause to evil: "Alive in triumph, and Mercutio slain? / Away to heaven respective lenity, / And fire-eyed fury be my conduct now!" (3.1.120–22). This is more hysteria than calculated evil, as has been much of his behavior throughout; but to make him a sympathetic character, Shakespeare must later show him in better light, for the audience would identify the vow as the most important speech in any play: that of moral choice.

Friar Laurence rightly rebukes him for his tantrum at banishment:

> Hold thy desperate hand:
> Art thou a man? Thy form cries out thou art:
> Thy tears are womanish; thy wild acts denote
> The unreasonable fury of a beast.
>
> (3.3.108–11)

It is the big Renaissance challenge. Romeo *will* become a man rather than beast. His heart becomes new opened. First it is through a human awareness of true, giving love. Then, as disaster comes, he resolves to follow Juliet in death. His first important recognition of other people besides Juliet is that of the starving apothecary in Mantua. In an otherwise needlessly long passage, Romeo sees suffering of a kind he has never known. The apothecary, "bare and full of wretchedness" (5.1.68), becomes a fellow member of humanity. So, more surprisingly, does the man who wants to supplant him in love. Hav-

ing, in self-defense, had to kill Paris at the graveyard, Romeo recognizes him almost with brotherhood: "O, give me thy hand, / One
writ with me in sour misfortune's book! / I'll bury thee in a triumphant grave" (5.3.81–83). Our improving feeling for Romeo, and his
innocence, is furthered by his most generally applicable statement.
After listening to the Friar's sage counsel, Romeo unanswerably expresses the almost insuperable divisiveness of the play: "Thou canst
not speak of that thou dost not feel" (3.3.64).

Those who must learn to feel and heal the dissension are not the
lovers but the old people (Tybalt, though a youth, doesn't stand a
chance). The major exception is Friar Laurence, who is the kindest,
wisest man. True, he cannot communicate his belief in reason over
passion, caution over haste, to the impassioned Romeo. But he has a
lovingly humorous relationship with the youth, as it is he who risks
his calling by agreeing that the hasty marriage may do some good.
More important, he understands, as few characters in Shakespeare do,
the human differences that even a union of mankind can have. In this
view, he is voicing an important credo for Shakespeare's tragedies.
The important speech is the friar's first utterance. Its narrative purpose is to show Friar Laurence's knowledge of herbs and thus prepare
for the potion he gives Juliet. Its larger purpose is to comment, dramatically and not didactically, upon the fundamental need for human
understanding that the tragedy will explore. In part he says:

> The earth that's nature's mother is her tomb.
> What is her burying grave, that is her womb;
> And from her womb children of divers kind
> We sucking on her natural bosom find,
> Many for many virtues excellent,
> None but for some and yet all different.
> O, mickle is the powerful grace that lies
> In plants, herbs, stones, and their true qualities;
> For nought so vile that on the earth doth live
> But to the earth some special good doth give;
> Nor ought so good but strained from that fair use
> Revolts from true birth, stumbling on abuse.
>   (2.3.9–20)

The Friar, in the fullest sense, is *aware*. It is the other older people
who have to learn that the hostile fragmentation of humanity is evil.
The Chorus is reaffirmed. Neither Romeo nor Juliet but the blindly
furious participants in the feud take the role of those who must learn.

One hesitates to explain the meaning of a Shakespearean tragedy by doctrine and not verbally in the text. But the sacrifice of innocent children for the punishment of sinful parents was one of the best-known lessons of the Bible. It radiates from St. Augustine to many other theologians and preachers. Augustine takes up the great "complaint" that innocent children should not suffer in "On Free Will": "By the torments of their children parents have their hard hearts softened, their faith exercised, and their tenderness proved."[3] Among the contemporary divines who drove home the message were Gervase Babington and James Pilkington. If one is resistant to the influences of sermons, the lines of another major poet may be more persuasive. Spenser writes of Prince Arthur in *The Faerie Queene:*

> Indeed (then said the prince) the evil donne
> Dyes not, when breathe the bodie first doth leave,
> But from the grandsyre to the nephewes sonne,
> And all his seed the curse doth often cleave
> Till vengeance utterly the guilt bereave:
> So streightly God doth judge.[4]

At the ending of *Romeo and Juliet,* the Prince, the ultimately authoritative speaker, drives home to the grief-stricken parents not a message of consolation but one of judgment. Addressing the "enemies" with especial, perhaps ironic emphasis, the Prince asks: "Where be these enemies? Capulet, Montague, / See what a scourge is laid upon your head, / That heaven finds means to kill your joys with love" (5.3.291–93). His conclusion is theologically precise and harsh: "All are punished" (5.3.295).

But the resolution that gives the play its final beauty and the audience the comfort without which it can scarcely endure shows the union of the fated houses. The formerly hard-hearted Capulet asks his "brother Montague" for his hand. "This is my daughter's jointure, for no more / Can I demand" (5.3.297). The marriage still exists, and the all-important blessing of the fathers is given. Each father, moreover, will raise a statue of the other's child in pure gold. Much, indeed, has been lost. But all passion, in a passionate play, where there has been much of hate but more of love, is spent. For the muted ending of such a tragedy—one set in a dark world momentarily ablaze with color and beauty—the Prince's solemn words are then appropriate: "A glooming peace this morning with it brings / The sun for sorrow will not show his head" (5.3.305–6).

Chapter Four
Julius Caesar

Classic Story

Like *Romeo and Juliet, Julius Caesar* is a classic play in that it draws deeply for its popular appeal from the wells of lasting and broad human issues. It is, however, classic in a stricter sense in that it is formal rather than romantic. There is not, despite tears, the heartrending sense of pity that audiences feel in the earlier love tragedy. There are only two female characters, the major of whom, Brutus's wife, Portia, seeks to be as strongly controlled as the stern politically minded men who completely dominate the play. It is a man's world—specifically heroic men of the classical Roman period. Yet despite its high-minded, often intellectual qualities, it has taken its place, like the preceding tragedy, among the staples of our education. There are few of us who have not memorized "Friends, Romans, countrymen, lend me your ears!" (3.2.73). And there are few of us who have not felt the attractiveness of Brutus; or responded to the fierce, only partially noble anger of Cassius, the chief motivating conspirator against Caesar; or reacted with mingled awe and distancing to great Caesar himself. Shakespeare has succeeded in making this popular, if not the most soul-wrenching, drama from classical history, and generally rendered it in a muted classical manner.

A major reason for the success of this Roman play is that for the first time Shakespeare drew upon perhaps his most important literary source, Plutarch's *Lives of the Noble Grecians and Romans,* in the superb Elizabethan translation of Sir Thomas North. The play was to be followed almost a decade later by two other similarly founded Roman works, *Antony and Cleopatra* and *Coriolanus.* These three are indebted not only to North's language but also to Plutarch's interest in character as it relates to state affairs. All three plays deal with men of stature, though their greatness is not alike, all sharing only political eminence, varying degrees of military prowess, and the testing of nobility.

Indeed, in *Julius Caesar* alone, there is doubt who the hero is. Caesar would for Elizabethans have been, at least by historical reputation, the loftiest man in the play; but here he is shown in the least impressive phase of his career—his final days—and he is, as noted, a baffling man to assess. He has still much grandeur; and even after he is cut down midway in the drama, his spirit is felt, finally returning as a ghost to torment and perhaps doom his beloved friend, Brutus, whose thrust of a dagger had been "the most unkindest cut of all" (3.2.183). But Shakespeare has made full sympathy for him difficult. He would be a king, an ambition abhorrent to the high-minded republican conspirators. Even more troublesome for us is his almost ridiculous hubris, his epileptic fits, his sterility, and a gratuitous blemish, his deafness in one ear.

Brutus, although ultimately a murderer of his fatherlike figure and though not so towering as a historical figure, is usually regarded as the hero. He is before us almost from beginning to end, and the final eloquent words are about him. He is most classically the Roman patriot putting "the general [good]" (2.1.12) before his valued self-control and his esteemed Caesar. He towers above the envious, selfishly motivated Cassius and the politic Mark Antony as a character study. Following a tendency that we have noted will be paramount in most of the tragedies, he suffers feelingly, and he learns and ultimately improves as a human being from his tragic ordeal.

Little more need be added here to remind most readers of the essentials of this moving, but restrained, story. Cassius persuades Brutus to join the supposedly high-principled conspirators. The "ides of March" find them cutting down "the foremost man in all the world" (4.2.22). Mark Antony, because of Brutus's insistence, is allowed to speak at Caesar's funeral, provided that he will not speak against the conspirators. So craftily and eloquently does he carry out his limited role that he fires the populace to mutiny. The killers must flee and prepare for battle with both Antony and the young Octavius Caesar. At Philippi, because of a never-resolved complex of causes, Brutus and Cassius are defeated and like true Romans commit suicide. The state, as always in Shakespeare, is brought together, but here only tenuously, with the promise of the installation of a new triumvirate—Octavius, Antony, and Lepidus.

Some Monstrous State

It has been suggested by S. F. Johnson that the most important "character" in *Julius Caesar* is the populace.[1] This is acceptable only if by the populace we mean the people, and by them, the state. Without going so far as to call this, as we would the English histories, a political play, certainly one of its most impressive features is the prominence of forces behind human endeavor. These forces are not tamely those of reasoned arguments about monarchy or republicanism. They are closer to, but more fully dramatized than, the star-crossed urban and domestic conflicts in *Romeo and Juliet*. Not only Rome, but also the coherence of order, seems to be in tumult. What Elyot and Hooker threatened about the violation of degree is at issue. Even more, perhaps, "the state of a man" (2.1.67), as Brutus puts it, "suffers then the nature of an insurrection" (2.1.68–69).

Shakespeare is experimenting, almost for the first time, with the fullest terms of the supernatural, with prophecies, omens, and what Thomas Nashe called, in a book of that title, "the terrors of the night" (1594). Cassius, complacent in his own self-righteousness, attributes these terrors to "some monstrous state" (1.3.71). Later plays will raise them to more than political upheavals. Indeed, the most powerful of the tragedies will have phenomena enlarging human matters to macrocosmic, apocalyptic concerns.

In *Julius Caesar*, Shakespeare presents—along with lions in the street, repeated tempests, alarums, "ghastly women" (1.3.23)—a sense of destiny. It is a transitional political era in which men seem compelled to take action and in which the major Shakespearean device of moral choice seems at times disturbingly threatened. A Soothsayer accurately warns Caesar of the ides of March. Calphurnia dreams, even with correct imagery, of the bloody slaughter of her husband. Caesar himself, who rejects as cowardice his staying home from the capitol, feels the force of destiny: "What can be avoided / Whose end is purposed by the mighty gods?" (2.2.27–28). And Brutus interprets the slaying of Caesar as inevitable: "'tis but the time / And drawing days out, that men stand upon" (3.1.99–100). In one of the best prophetic "mirror scenes," an otherwise irrelevant character, Cinna, makes us aware of a compulsive force toward action. Dreaming that he feasted with Caesar, he sadly reflects: "I have no will to wonder forth of doors, / Yet something leads me forth" (3.3.3–4). Trying vainly to persuade the crazed populace that he is Cinna the poet and not Cinna the conspirator, he has his heart torn from his body. We shall see that, in addition to Calphurnia's dream of Caesar's heart, this symbol is eloquent through much of the play.

Besides episodes such as these, major characters reflect upon fate in some of Shakespeare's most beautifully somber language—language of a poetry that gives a welcome eloquence to what has often been considered a stylistically cold play. Cassius, who at first ridicules the compulsion of destiny, chides Brutus's fatalism in some of the most quoted words in the play: "Men at some time are masters of their fates. / The fault, dear Brutus, is not in our stars, / But in ourselves, that we are underlings." (1.2.139–40). These lines are confident and only partially troubled in their strength. But as Cassius experiences the forces that even so strongly willed a man as he may undergo, his language takes on an eloquent sadness. Near the battle of Philippi, he asks Messala to witness that against his will he is compelled to set upon one battle all his "liberties": "You know that I held Epicurus strong / And his opinion. Now I change my mind / And partly credit things that do presage" (5.1.75–78). He then relates movingly the omens of the birds that first encouraged his powers and now reject them. He feels also a tragic pattern in his life: "This day I breathed first. Time is come round, / And where I did begin, there shall I end. / My life has run his compass" (5.3.23–25).

Brutus, a more sadly troubled man, also loses what sense he first had of controlling his fate. Like Cassius, but more movingly and with more philosophical depth, he first rejects suicide. He considers it cowardly and vile to avoid "the time of life"—"Arming myself with patience / To stay the providence of some high powers / That govern us below" (5.1.105–7). "Arming," to one not as Stoic as Brutus is, connotes a hardened kind of self-fortifying, and we shall see that this is a barrier to fullest feeling. But Brutus is by no means insensitive.[2] He simply knows "my hour is come" (5.5.20). And while eager to "know / The end of this day's business ere it comes" (5.1.122–23), he is suggestive of a greater subsequent hero in ultimately acquiescing: "But it sufficeth that the day will end, / And then the end is known" (5.1.124–25). Incessant "low alarums," or muffled drums, underscore potently the inevitable advancing doom.

Tragic Mission

Assuming, as we must, that Brutus is the hero of the play, we must also wonder why Shakespeare placed so meditative, analytical a man in a play overhung with destiny that tragically frustrates man's endeavor. In *Romeo and Juliet,* the principals are also victims of a star-crossed and even evil state. But they are not mentally capable of being agents of their fortunes. Brutus, it is true, has opportunities for crucial decisions, including not killing Antony and advancing to battle at Philippi.

He above all has a decision, so placed and so emphasized that it may well be a fatally wrong moral choice, of whether to join the conspiracy. This decision is made in the famous "orchard soliloquy," beginning with:

> It must be by his death; and for my part,
> I know no personal cause to spurn at him,
> But for the general. He would be crowned.
> How that might change his nature, there's the question.
>
> (2.1.10–13)

Readers familiar with Shakespeare's next tragedy, *Hamlet,* may be forgiven for seeing in "there's the question" an anticipation of "That is the question." Both occur in soliloquies—speeches often revelatory of deeply reflective natures. But for the moment we must acknowledge that Brutus is wrong. His self-questioning of his motives is marred by sophistry. Whether this conclusion, like other fatal decisions in the play (including that by the poet Cinna), is due to fate, we cannot be sure, for Cassius is probably right in saying that "men *at some time* are masters of their fate" (1.2.139, emphasis added). What we can say more confidently is that for the first time Shakespeare made an intellectual his hero and did so in a play less hospitable to intellectuals than to mountebanks like Antony, to mobs, and especially to "a monstrous state." And for the first time, with subsequent triumph in *Hamlet,* Shakespeare placed before a reluctant hero an incongenial mission. He is the first hero for whom action does not come easily; in this respect, Brutus contrasts sharply with the just-created Henry V, perhaps Shakespeare's last "man of action."

Not only the orchard soliloquy but much of the preassassination action of the play is devoted to Brutus undergoing an intellectual ordeal. He cannot join the early celebration of Caesar ("the order of the course," 1.2.25), for he is not "gamesome" and lacks "some part of that quick spirit that is Antony" (1.2.28–29). When Cassius blames him for not having "that gentleness / and show of love as I was wont to have" (1.1.33–34), Brutus pleads his divided mind. He is "with himself at war" (1.2.46) and vexed with conflicting passions ("passions of some difference," 1.2.40). The early Brutus is at his most appealing to us when he undergoes the agony of indecision. How he has suffered during this period is made the more persuasive after the orchard soliloquy by the self-description that Shakespeare has put into memorable words:

> Since Cassius first did whet me against Caesar
> I have not slept.
> Between the acting of a dreadful thing
> And the first motion [i.e., proposal], all the interim is
> Like a phantasm or a hideous dream.
> The genius and the mortal instrument
> Are then in council, and the state of a man,
> Like to a little kingdom, suffers then
> The nature of an insurrection.
>
> (2.1.61–69)

The reference in the first line to Cassius's seductive role alerts us to a familiar trait in Shakespeare's most attractive heroes: their noble vulnerability to smaller, craftier men. These men take an influential role in Brutus's early suffering and the later debasing of his character when he stabs Caesar. Like the typical seducing villain in Shakespeare, Cassius informs the audience of his part in Brutus's decision:

> Well, Brutus, thou art noble; yet I see
> Thy honorable mettle may be wrought
> From that it is disposed. Therefore it is meet
> That noble minds keep ever with their likes;
> For who so firm that cannot be seduced?
>
> (1.2.305–9)

"Nobility" in its common Shakespearean connotation is an admirable but dangerous trait. Men who possess it are unfit to mingle with the base. Othello is "the noble Moor" (*Oth* 2.3.132), Coriolanus is "too noble for the world" (*Cor* 3.1.255). Brutus will eventually prevail in reputation as "the noblest Roman of them all" (5.5.68). But there will be the debasement of the middle of the play. In testing Brutus's true mettle, Shakespeare will make a major part of the action the examination not only of his honorable mind but also of his heart.

Our Hearts You See Not

An important theme of *Julius Caesar* is emotional awakening. In the first scene, the tribunes move the populace to "weep your tears"

(1.1.58) for their guilt in forgetting Pompey in honoring Caesar. "See," they craftily gloat, "whe'r their basest mettle be not moved" (1.1.61). Antony is a more complex and much more important orator to the people. His funeral orations are designed to "move / The stones of Rome" (3.2.299–30). This he superbly does, with a disturbing mixture of mountebank and genuine griever. Probably no other character in Shakespeare so successfully awakens pity and tears. "I perceive," he tells the mob, "you feel / The dint of pity. These are gracious drops" (3.2.193–94). And he can weep too, spontaneously, as he sees tears in the messenger from Octavius. Brutus, "an honorable man" (3.2.82), also appeals to the feelings of the people. His defense of his murderous action is, however, sterner than Antony's, demanding of others the sacrificial choice he has imposed upon himself.

Yet it is questionable whether he is colder than Antony. He does not seem to move himself so dramatically as Antony or even Cassius does, perhaps, as has been suggested, because he has "armed" (1.3.114) himself. He also has a more low-keyed, meditative temper, one that resists exposing his feelings. He apologizes early to Cassius, who tries to strike a "show of fire" (1.2.177) from him:

> Cassius,
> Be not deceived. If I have veiled my look,
> I turn the trouble of my countenance
> Merely upon myself.
>
> (1.2.36–39)

We finally are prepared to defend him from Cassius's telling charge: "Brutus, this sober form of yours hides wrongs" (4.2.40).

But rescuing his sober hero from too much control in order to engage our approval meant for Shakespeare a real challenge. For the almost formal execution of his great benefactor moves us, even without Antony's help, as does almost no other action in the play. Had Brutus slain him in passion, the fault might have appeared less. There is too much ritual in Brutus's staging of the killing.[3] We draw back in horror from the bathing of arms in Caesar's blood. We are not mollified by his promise to give reasons to Antony "Why and wherein Caesar was dangerous" (3.1.222), for his answer betrays a ritualistic concept of his action: "Or else were this a savage spectacle" (3.1.223). We suddenly see what seems to be the cold cruelty of the "spectacle" when Antony refers to "these butchers" (3.1.255). Brutus had never thought of himself as such.

There is, then, a real danger that the proud Roman Stoic will alienate us, as he would an Elizabethan audience, by doing what we noticed in chapter 1 as "setting a presse on the heart." Brutus never quite clears himself of the taint of a hardening heart. Possibly Shakespeare meant for him to embody the current mixed feelings about the Stoics.[4] But Brutus does, as we somehow want him to, ultimately vindicate his humanity. Certain episodes, if examined together, prove this rehabilitation and also—lest we place philosophy before drama—the moving close to the play.

The most obvious explanation of Brutus's lack of emotion is, as we have noted, a deeply held belief (for it is strong enough to be more than a beseeming conduct) in having emotion but not exhibiting it. The importance of this belief is apparent in his strongly urged directions to his fellow conspirators:

> Good gentlemen, look fresh and merrily.
> Let not our looks put on our purposes,
> But bear it as our Roman actors do,
> With untired spirits and formal constancy.
> (2.1.224–27)

The genuineness of this advice, and the feeling beneath it, is effectively proved in the soliloquy that immediately follows. It begins with his attempt to summon his boy, Lucius, who is sound asleep. This action emphasizes the redeeming quality in Brutus, often mentioned, that he cannot sleep:

> Enjoy the honey-heavy dew of slumber.
> Thou has no figures nor no fantasies
> Which busy care draws in the brains of men;
> Therefore thou sleep'st so sound.
> (2.1.230–33)

Beneath his seeming composure, we must always be aware of poetic "figures" and "fantasies." Like many of Shakespeare's heroes, he suffers more because he is a poet; but the "formal constancy" (2.1.227) of his speech obscures for too many readers the tension latent in it.

A still greater instance of his belief in concealing the heart occurs when, with bloody hands, he must confront Antony:

> O Antony, beg not your death of us!
> Though now we must appear bloody and cruel,
> As by our hands and this our present act
> You see we do, yet see you but our hands
> And this the bleeding business they have done.
> Our hearts you see not. They are pitiful.
> $\qquad$ (3.1.164–69)

And he promises Antony—a man unworthy of a promise because he disguises rather than holds his heart—"our hearts / Of brothers' temper, do receive you in / With all kind love" (3.1.174–76).

The underlying and essentially undying humanity of Brutus is equally evident in other episodes. One, an early one, shows him in a charming, revealing argument with Portia. She pleads with him to divulge the cause of his "ungentle" (2.1.242), troubled behavior. And in doing so, she provides us with a unique vision of the very human Brutus that only a wife can know. In this view he lacks the proud control that he manages with men. He scratches his head, impatiently stamps his foot, and angrily waves her away. Yet he loves her tenderly and immediately redeems himself in our eyes when he protests to Portia: "You are my true and honorable wife, / As dear to me as the ruddy drops / That visit my sad heart" (2.1.288–90). Brutus has, one might say, chosen a life of the "sad heart." He fails to see the comedy of his behavior and has no sense of humor (the play is, compared with other tragedies, uniquely short on comedy). He has no small talk and no small interests. What he loves about Portia is her courage (she seeks his respect by wounding her thigh) and her nobility: "O ye gods, / Render me worthy of this noble wife!" (2.1.302–3). And he will ultimately prove himself worthy in a way of which she would approve.

His relation with Cassius, his "brother" (4.2.37), is almost that of lovers, and the dramatic quarrel scene between them reveals even more tellingly a less formal Brutus. Cassius, accused by Brutus of taking bribes, protests that his friend does not love him. Brutus, too, feels that Cassius's love is not genuine but has begun to decay into an "enforced ceremony" (4.2.21) proper to "hollow men" (4.2.23). At first, both men in this late and hence important scene appear to disadvantage. Guilt—as Shakespeare often uses this universal maxim—always separates. It also makes exalted behavior difficult. In this lovers' quarrel, a fundamental selfishness and pettiness surfaces, particularly in Cassius. But it is he who, more passionate, helps to end the quarrel (which Brutus had typically directed into his tent) by offering his friend his dagger and his heart, "dearer than Pluto's mine, richer than gold" (4.3.102). Brutus, for his part, shows constantly higher ideals, refusing to rob the poor of their money. But his most persuasive nobility and humanity in ending the quarrel begins with his almost naked confession: "O Cassius, I am sick of many griefs" (4.3.144). When Cassius chides him for not using his philosophy and for giving way to "accidental evil" (4.3.146), Brutus forever redeems himself with "No man bears sorrow better. Portia is dead" (4.3.147). Even Cassius must confess that he could not have so borne himself. Shakespeare, for some reason, duplicates the news of Portia's death, possibly because it is so important. When Messala tells Brutus of his loss, Brutus reveals what we should never forget about him, that his sad heart has perforce controlled display, by meditating upon the worst that may befall him: "With meditating that she must die once, I have the patience to endure it now" (4.3.191–92). And finally defeated, "a noble vessel full of grief," Brutus "meditates" (5.4.12,13).

Scattered instances in his favor follow, notably an apparently trivial scene with his boy, Lucius. It is clearly a "mirror scene," for it does not advance the plot but tells us much about Brutus's "gentleness," a quality mentioned centrally in Antony's eulogy (5.5.73). He asks the sleepy boy to play for him. When the boy falls asleep and the music ceases, the fated, weary Brutus is given one of the most feelingly lyrical speeches in the play:

> This is a sleepy tune. O murd'rous slumber!
> Layest thou thy leaden mace upon my boy,
> That plays thee music? Gentle knave, goodnight.
> I will not do thee so much harm to wake thee.
> If thou dost nod, thou break'st thy instrument;
> I'll take it from thee; and, good boy, goodnight.
> (4.3.267–72)

The solicitous tenderness of these words, in a night of suffering, is more revelatory of true feeling than all of Antony's oratory. Yet it is meaningful that Antony should be allowed to speak definitively for the dead Brutus. Antony may not, as Caesar says of Cassius, be the

most able to look quite through the deeds of men. But he has more
perspective and humanity. Cassius would not unskeptically consider
Brutus the noblest Roman of them all. Nor could he fully appreciate
that

> All the conspirators save only he
> Did that they did in envy of great Caesar.
> He, only in a general honest thought
> And common good to all, made one of them.
>   (5.5.69–72)

Certainly, the finale of Antony's eulogy is the choric tribute that we
need, for it recognizes Brutus's broad (if not always displayed) humanity: "His life was gentle, and the elements / So mixed in him that
Nature might stand up / And say to all the world, 'This was a man'"
(5.5.73–75). Although, then, this is a classic play, a Renaissance audience would have thrilled to these lines. They are the highest possible tribute to human character, and applicable to men like Sidney
and, perhaps (as Ben Jonson in part testifies), to Shakespeare himself.

Chapter Five
Hamlet

Revenge Tradition and the Noble Mind

As the world's most famous play, *Hamlet* draws upon an almost shameless quantity of popular themes. Most of these, moreover, are sensational and sufficient to compel the groundlings to stand throughout Shakespeare's longest play. But the revenge tradition that underlies it, and that gives it gripping excitement, would have struck contemporary audiences as profoundly different from such bloody tragedies as they were used to. It was a hero who, because of his sensitive, moral nature, suffers keenly from his task. His is, as both his loved Ophelia and his friend Horatio say, a noble mind; and all evidence points to his reluctance to be cruel in order to be kind. The play for succeeding audiences has consequently become more than a simple revenge play: it has become archetypal as the ordeal of taking repulsive but occasionally passionate action. "It is *we*," wrote William Hazlitt, "who are Hamlet."[1] And Coleridge acknowledged, "I have a smack of Hamlet, if I may say so."[2] Few of us cannot identify with the hero, and many are the warm discussions about what is his "mystery" (3.2.352). Not only students, lay people, and troubled souls have argued about the melancholy Dane; psychoanalysts have also generously donated their services to unravel probably the most complex character in literature.

But we must not underestimate, however crude it may be, the underlying revenge tradition. It gives to the play not only plot but also what we have called the tragedy of passion. Indeed, Hamlet's words to his only friend, Horatio—"Give me that man / That is not passion's slave" (3.2.68–69)—express one of the main struggles that Hamlet himself must undergo. For this tradition, Shakespeare draws mainly upon Seneca, partly upon *The Spanish Tragedy,* and also upon a cruder anonymous version of the play, now known as the *UrHamlet,* no longer extant. Moreover, Shakespeare draws upon almost all of the horrendous elements of the tradition. Hamlet is summoned by the ghost of his father to avenge his death at the hands of his brother

Claudius. He sinks into a deep sadness, close at times to madness, in his mission. His already sick mind is sullied by sex—notably the incest of his mother, who has married Claudius within a month or two of the funeral. Not especially Senecan are the episodes involving Polonius's family, notably Ophelia and her tragic love for Hamlet, though her madness and probable suicide are partly in the tradition. More conventional are Hamlet's delay (though not its psychological causes) and his cunning concern to make the revenge as appropriate and condign as possible. The play-within-the-play, which Hamlet devises to "catch the conscience of the king" (2.2.590–91), is surely an exploitation of the popular episode in *The Spanish Tragedy*. Many of the subsequent violent elements—the murder of Polonius, the leaping into Ophelia's grave, the fatal duel with Laertes, the accidental poisoning of Gertrude, and the ultimate, condign slaying of Claudius—are variations upon the revenge tradition. But those elements that would have most pleased and been recognized by the audience are the burden of revenge, the ghost, madness, incest, delay, and appropriateness in technique of revenge. What the audience would have witnessed with wonder are the philosophical extensions of cruel finesse and passion. These extensions, attributable largely to the noble and brooding mind of the revenger, are well expressed by him as "thoughts beyond the reaches of our souls" (1.4.56). In them recrimination for delay takes the form of self-analysis and of anguished reflection upon the state of man that have scarcely been excelled.

As in *Julius Caesar,* the play that probably preceded it by only a year, the protagonist is of a noble, philosophical mind. Shakespeare found compellingly interesting during these years—and probably never again—a protagonist who is not primarily of heroic stature. (Bradley, intent upon making all four of the major heroes awesomely large, had to attribute to Hamlet "genius," and Bradley could not have done even that for Brutus.) These two are men of conscience and thought who have placed upon them an incongenial burden, made even more intolerable by the crude environment that produces it.

In placing Hamlet in the revenge tradition, we must seek to correct the common stereotype that critics who depend upon this tradition make of Hamlet's revenge. Hamlet's task is not so simple as killing the king. His, rather, is the most profound kind of revenge (if one can justly call it that) imposed upon any hero. His task is to set the times right, to purge the court of Elsinore. This duty, then, is much more profound in yet another sense than revenge tragedy.

The play concerns the purging, partly by revenge, of a corrupt society. Hamlet must make of man more than a beast. And in doing so, he must constantly struggle not to be a beast himself, not to let his noble mind be overthrown, not to lose his "capability and godlike reason" (4.4.38), not to let his heart lose its nature.

The Court of Elsinore

Most of the action in *Hamlet* takes place in the Court of Elsinore, which appears first in the second scene. Superficially, especially after the bleak, heartsick fear of the opening scene, set at midnight on the battlements and terrorizing not only the sentries but also the skeptical Horatio with two appearances of the Ghost, it seems to be a warm, bright, and civilized setting. After the midnight out-of-doors darkness—a darkness emphasized by Marcellus's opening and unanswered question to the seemingly void universe as well as to Francisco, "Who's there?" (1.1.1)—it is an indoor scene full of color and fine dress. Claudius, from the throne, reassuringly, brilliantly brings the newly formed state together. He logically explains the hasty marriage and the "mirth in funeral" (1.2.12). He warmly deals with his supporter-counselor Polonius, and genially gives his counselor's son, Laertes, permission to go to Paris. The threatened invasion of Fortinbras is expertly dealt with. Only Hamlet, a man on whom rests what G. Wilson Knight calls "the embassy of death,"[3] remains darkly alone, unresponsive to warm, reasonable consolation and a proffered stature as a son. Hamlet, who will prove to be the most difficult stepson in literature, answers only his mother's plea to stay in Denmark, and even she does not escape his scathing wit.

On the whole, however, it seems to be a comfortable court. And scene 3 stresses this impression by bringing together in close intimacy Polonius and his family. Laertes gives words of worldly, experienced caution to protect his sister's virtue, but affection is shown even in her bantering reply to Paris-bound Laertes. Polonius then arrives and gives, in a celebrated father-to-son speech, counsel on a prudent but gentlemanly life. The most important function of the scene is the restraint placed upon Ophelia in not seeing Hamlet. He will but trifle with her, or "wreck" (2.1.113) her. Hamlet, of a noble nature free from all contriving, is later severely shaken by the narrow vision of the restraint and the close-heartedness that it represents. It is, all in all, a scene and a family not untypical of the court as, in more insidious and corrupt forms, we shall generally see it. It is narrow, politic, suspicious—a prison that does not have, like Hamlet, "a heart unfortified" (1.2.96).

Yet, even without the Italianate villainy of Claudius, it is a court that will somehow merit the scourging of a terrible kind. Typical again are the character and fate of Polonius's family, which to a person will be wiped out. To grasp the true nature of Elsinore, and the purgation that it will receive, we must not begin with Claudius or Polonius or the premature settling of a disturbed state. We must not begin with a sophisticated indoor scene. These scenes are often, as *As You Like It* and *King Lear* illustrate, less close to reality than the scenes set in the forest or on the heath. We must, in short, begin the play as Shakespeare does, at midnight on the battlements; with characters confronting without pretense or control the raw evil, the rottenness of the state of Denmark.

This Bodes Some Strange Eruption to the State

Many modern productions of the play omit, with serious consequences, the entire first scene. Their reasoning may be practical, for drastic cuts are necessary in Shakespeare's longest play. But a fundamental misunderstanding of the play is also likely. It is a scene that, as Horatio explains, "is prologue to the omen coming on," sent by "heaven and earth together" (1.1.123,124). Horatio likens it to the prodigious events preceding the death of Caesar. A state is in jeopardy, and to the Elizabethans that threat of war meant that a sin-sick land is to be scourged. This first scene describes at length the preparations against an invasion by Fortinbras, who is also omitted from many productions, even though he will appear prominently at the end of the play. True, the Ghost will appear with his "dread command" (3.4.109) in the fifth scene, but he is needed at the start by his position to dominate the state's peril and to give, like Fortinbras, a military beginning as well as a military ending to the play. He terrifies not just because he is a ghost but also because he comes in the "warlike form / In which the majesty of buried Denmark / Did sometimes march" (1.1.47–49). He is the only ghost in extant Elizabethan drama to appear in armor. He deserves the first scene—even without Hamlet—to sound the note of the dominant theme of doom.

Long and soft peace was not an auspicious condition in Elizabethan thought. Military theorists and theologians warned repeatedly that its symptoms were those of a sinful and sick land, ripe for sacking. There is an excessive softness in Claudius's kingdom, a peace-bred decadence. The new king differs markedly from his martial brother. All the parasites of peace here have proliferated: courtiers—sinister and suave like Claudius, politic like Laertes, false like Rosencrantz and Guildenstern, or effete like Osric; corrupt lawyers and impeded justice; artful and affected language; in fact all the decadent types and qualities mentioned in Hamlet's most famous soliloquy. More serious still are the moral corruptions of a peacetime state threatened by corrective war: sexual aberrations and license (extending to Laertes and to the recurrent image of the harlot); social disease imaged by "impostume" (4.4.27) and "canker" (5.2.69); the "oppressor's wrong" (3.1.71); "rank" (1.2.136; many times emphasized, often by Hamlet, and connoting sexual stench); and gross debauchery in such forms as heavy drinking, usually and ominously conjoined with the sound of cannon.

Imagery, as we have noticed, goes deeper than "seems" (1.2.75–76), the picture of Elsinore given in the second scene. Without dwelling upon the well-known disease images catalogued by Caroline Spurgeon,[4] we readily recall such dominant expressions of physical deterioration as "the fatness of these pursy times" (3.4.154) and "the drossy age" (5.2.181). Especially basic to the play is a hidden kind of disease, sometimes discovered too late. This kind of image is unmistakably related to peace-bred corruption in one of the most important and overlooked passages in the play (it is overlooked in productions because the scene in which it appears is usually cut). Hamlet comments upon the appearance of Fortinbras's army as follows: "This is th'impostume of much wealth and peace, / That inward breaks, and shows no cause without / Why the man dies" (4.4.27–29). Barnabe Riche (an author whose *Farewell to Militarie Profession* Shakespeare read) indicates the specific kinds of inward rottenness concealed in peacetime: deceit, fraud, flattery, incontinence, inordinate lust, and "to be short . . . al manner of filthinesse."[5] Riche, moreover, got his diagnosis from a respected authority: St. Augustine in *The City of God*.

In fact, most alarms to England had theological origins, based upon biblical analogues and hence most terrifying to Elizabethans. Babylon, Sodom, and Gomorrah were cities especially subject to visitation of armed portents: but the sinful city that compellingly caught the horrified attention of England was Jerusalem before its destruc-

tion by Titus. Was there no way in which military devastation could
be avoided? In a sermon called *Gods Mercies and Jerusalems Miseries,*
Lancelot Dawes expounds the text from Jeremiah 5:1. The text is to
search in the city for a man "that executeth Judgment and seeketh
the truth and I will spare it." Only one man, it is emphasized, need
be found. Such a minister of judgment must be able to give drastic
physic to the moral disease of the city, for "from the sole of her foot
to the crown of her head, there be nothing found in her but wounds
and swelling, and sores full of corruption."[6]

Such a man is not to be found in Jerusalem. Nineveh, however,
was redeemed, and its redemption was found in many a sermon. But
its success on the stage is more significant of popular appeal and helps
clarify the meaning of *Hamlet* to its audience. In *A Looking-Glass for
London and England,* Thomas Lodge and Robert Greene dramatized
the frightening sins of a city under a sensual monarch, the appearance
of an angel who brings in Jonas and Oseas as prophets to scourge the
court repeatedly with moral warnings, and finally the internal purgation of the city within the appointed forty days.

If we consider Hamlet to be, like Jonas and Oseas, a wildly
speaking voice of judgment and correction, we may be struck by
other parallels between the two plays. Rasni, the king, "loves cham-
bering and wantonesse," indulges in carousing, and rules a kingdom
of "filthinesses and sinne." He is theatened: "The foe shall pierce the
gates with iron rampes."[7] The most arresting specific parallel is that
Rasni falls sensually in love with, and marries, his own sister.

Hamlet is too complex a play, and Hamlet too various a character,
to fit comfortably into any tradition. One must, however, attempt to
account for as many of its images as possible, especially if these give
the play and its hero a significance greater than killing a king, or
suffering from delay, or meaningless abuse of others, or near madness.

O Heart, Lose Not Thy Nature

Hamlet, as a corrective surrogate form of war in Denmark, wages
a still more crucial war as an instrument of destiny. He is a human
being, one who must battle within himself a war in itself, a war between ruthlessness (a terrible passion) and humane feelings. The
Ghost, in his story to his son, tells him not to pity him but to take
stern action. The early Hamlet, though sickeningly bitter at his

mother's perfidy and the "bloat" (3.4.183) king's lust, is mostly a noble mind, one not, despite Ophelia's words, yet overthrown. Near the end of the play, when he has killed Polonius, he can be heartless—"Thou wretched, rash, intruding fool, farewell! / I took thee for thy better" (3.4.32–33); this is the only elegy he can pronounce over the dead father of his once beloved—and there is bestiality in his "I'll lug the guts into the neighbor room" (3.4.213). Perhaps, however, his most insightful view of the murder is a resignedly philosophical one:

> For this same lord,
> I do repent; but heaven hath pleased it so,
> To punish me with this, and this with me,
> That I must be their scourge and minister.
> (3.4.173–76)

The two key words are *scourge* and *minister*. The latter is an untainted agent of God. In *Richard III,* the virtuous Richmond on the eve of battle prays to God, "Make us thy ministers of chastisement" (*R3* 5.3.314). A scourge, on the other hand, has taken on himself revenge, like Tamburlaine, and is ultimately doomed. Such, at any rate, is the view of Fredson Bowers.[8] But the two words are often used interchangeably in the religious literature of the day, and Hamlet must, though he does not at first kill, behave with the cruelty of a scourge in setting the time right.

He is not, even from the beginning, temperamentally suited for a dispassionate enlightening of the moral sense of his mother, Ophelia, Polonius, or other tainted attendants at Elsinore. Once, doubtless, he had been. But when we first see him he is morbidly disillusioned with life and man ("man delights not me," 2.2.305) and woman. All is rank. Exacerbating his world view is the dread command of the ghost. This command, with its clinical account of his sexual mother, renders him incapable of a reasoned correction of others. The Ghost's command that usurps all else is "Let not the royal bed of Denmark be / A couch of luxury and damned incest" (1.5.82–83). This order makes for the savage attempt to mortify and chasten even so virtuous a girl as Ophelia.

More important, it makes him partly blind to the purging that his victims are undergoing of their own nature. Polonius, on his own, knows, as he places the book of devotion in Ophelia's hands, that

> We are oft to blame in this,
> 'Tis too much proved, that with devotion's visage
> And pious action, we do sugar o'er
> The devil himself.
>
> (3.1.46–49)

And even Claudius himself has his conscience wrung by this observation, for in an aside he virtually cries out:

> O, 'tis true.
> How smart a lash that speech doth give my conscience!
> The harlot's cheek, beautied with plast'ring art,
> Is not more ugly to the thing that helps it
> Than is my deed to my most painted word.
> O heavy burthen!
>
> (3.1.49–54)

Claudius is, however, more caught in conscience by Hamlet's play-within-the-play. His great soliloquy makes him more than a one-dimensional villain. He prays for the most-needed virtue in the play (perhaps in Shakespeare)—an open heart:

> Help, angels! Make assay.
> Bow, stubborn knees, and, heart with strings of steel,
> Be soft as sinews of the new-born babe.
> All may be well.
>
> (3.3.69–72)

Indeed a major aspect of Hamlet's excoriating mission is that even while it threatens to narrow his own heart and humanity (witness his callousness toward the death of Rosencrantz and Guildenstern), it awakens feelings of guilt in his victims.

Gertrude, morally obtuse, is his major obstacle in enlightenment, even as she is (though not in Freudian interpretation) the powerful threat to his role as minister rather than scourge. At once one of the most important and most enigmatic passages in the play is the Ghost's command concerning her:

> But howsomever thou pursuest this act,
> Taint not thy mind, nor let thy soul contrive
> Against thy mother ought. Leave her to heaven

> And to those thorns that in her bosom lodge
> To prick and sting her.
>
> (1.5.84–88)

Perhaps "Taint not thy mind" applies to the entire revenge mission, and in following that injunction Hamlet is reasonably successful. But the sexual nausea with which he views and treats his mother makes him almost hysterically and carnally passionate. When he is going to his mother's chambers at her request for the "closet scene," he must try to fortify his heart: "Soft, now to my mother. / O heart, lose not thy nature; let not ever / The soul of Nero enter this firm bosom" (3.2.377–79). So distraught is he, yet so anxious to carry out the Ghost's commands and his own deep feelings for Gertrude, that the scene is one of the most powerfully poetic in the play, despite its painfully sexual nature. It is also a crucial scene in that it carries out, in the largest sense, the ultimatum of the Ghost's charge: "Let not the royal bed of Denmark be / A couch for luxury and damned incest" (1.5.82–83). *Luxury,* it will be remembered, kept its Latin and romance meaning of licentiousness, of rank abundance, and of sumptuous pleasure, suitable to a kingdom of decadent peace.

Largely upon this scene, therefore, and not upon the killing of Claudius, depends the cleansing of what is rotten in the state of Denmark. And Hamlet succeeds through his brutal yet ardently moving rhetoric. He cries to Gertrude:

> Leave wringing of your hands. Peace, sit you down
> And let me wring your heart, for so I shall
> If it be made of penetrable stuff,
> If damned custom have not brazed it so
> That it is proof and bulwark against sense.
>
> (3.4.35–39)

So broad reaching, he cries, is her deed, that

> Heaven's face does glow,
> And this solidity and compound mass,
> With heated visage, as against the doom,
> Is thought-sick at the act.
>
> (3.4.49–52)

In effect, Hamlet correctly sees the earth as sick against the coming of the "doom." He is carrying out the fullest meaning of the Ghost's

command, a meaning in which Gertrude's vileness and subsequent
recognition are central. With a persistent battle between passionate
morality and morbid sexual revulsion in his soul, he pictures for her
the stench and sweat of her sexual nature:

> Nay, but to live
> In the rank sweat of an enseamed bed,
> Stewed in corruption, honeying and making love
> Over the nasty sty—
>
> (3.4.92–95)

She pleads with him to stop: "O Hamlet, thou hast cleft my heart in
twain" (3.4.157). In so confessing, she becomes (if we except Laertes)
the last and certainly most important sinner whose heart Hamlet has
opened.

The cruelty and even filth of his tactics make it sometimes questionable whether he fulfills his mission untainted. His earlier cruel
wit may be written off as "antic disposition" (1.5.172) as may his
"wild and whirling words" (1.5.133) used to his old friends. He is
probably right, in so intolerable a corrective role, to see himself as
both scourge and minister.

But, as we must more deeply recognize, Hamlet is *our* hero because, although forced into cruelty and even sadism, he is one of the
most beautiful in soul of any man Shakespeare created. We remember
mainly his heartrending soliloquies and his suffering. None but he
could speak words like

> To die, to sleep—
> No more—and by a sleep to say we end
> The heartache, and the thousand natural shocks
> That flesh is heir to.
>
> (3.1.60–63)

He may say that the deaths of Rosencrantz and Guildenstern "are not
near my conscience; their defeat / Does by their own insinuation
grow" (5.2.58–59). But, again, he can apologize humbly to the murderous Laertes, and he can go beyond his own plight when he states
that "by the image of my cause I see / The portraiture of his"
(5.2.77–78).

Still more in his favor is the concern for all human agony in his
soliloquies; and still more, the religious commitment that comes to

him after the hectic fever of his scourging. He learns: "There's a divinity that shapes our ends, / Rough-hew them how we will" (5.2.10–11). As his doom draws near, we see more of his own and not the age's suffering: "But thou wouldst not think how ill all's here about my heart" (5.2.201). Perhaps his first unselfish recognition is expressed in the biblical parable: "There is a special providence in the fall of a sparrow" (5.2.208–9).

With consummate artistry, therefore, Shakespeare is able to make the final scene of his most spiritually endowed hero twofold. Hamlet has earned, first, the beautiful tribute of Horatio, a man not given to unrealistic statements: "Now cracks a noble heart. Good night, sweet prince, / And flights of angels sing thee to thy rest" (5.2.348–49). And secondly, but not usually shown, is the conclusion expressed by Fortinbras, a conclusion representing *his* highest tribute. He had come to claim his "rights of memory in the kingdom" (5.2.378), though really to carry out a scourge that he himself does not know the basis for. He orders:

> Let four captains
> Bear Hamlet like a soldier to the stage,
> For he was likely, had he been put on,
> To have proved most royal; and for his passage
> The soldiers' music and the rights of war
> Speak loudly for him.
>
> (5.2.384–89)

The last sounds are of cannon, not for Claudius, but for Hamlet and regenerate Denmark.

Chapter Six
Othello

Little of This Great World Can I Speak

One of the miracles of Shakespeare's art is his infinite variety in the kind and credibility of the characters he creates. Seemingly compelled to explore new aspects of humanity, he never duplicates a major character. Only by such a recognition as this can we explain his turning from a thoughtful protagonist like Brutus or, more inexplicably, from a brilliant and brilliantly articulate mind like Hamlet's to the mind and world of Othello for his next tragic hero.

Hamlet must have given Shakespeare much satisfaction. He was a man into whose mind Shakespeare could put thoughts beyond the reaches of our souls, who could speak of the mystery of man, who could give unparalleled words to his own—and often mankind's—predicament. In his unburdened state he had been "The courtier's, soldier's, scholar's eye, tongue, sword" (*Ham* 3.1.151), and throughout the play he remains the wondered-at aristocrat. As is the case in Shakespeare's most troubling tragedies, *Hamlet* is given the added dimension of the supernatural, making possible speculation on the macrocosm as well as on earthbound man.

In turning to the person and story of Othello, Shakespeare made perhaps the most sudden turnabout in his career of writing tragedies. Though scarcely the "barbarian" (1.3.353) he is called, the Moor is emphatically black, probably rough, even fearsome, in appearance, and a foreign mercenary from Mouritania in refined Venice. Though of royal blood, since the age of seven he had a restrictive, painful life, being sold into slavery and spending most of his life in "the tented field" (1.3.85).

His "occupation" (3.3.357), to a degree found in no other Shakespearean hero, is war. He can therefore speak of the great world little "more than pertains to feats of broil and battle" (1.3.87). But that he loves the gentle Desdemona, he would not have given up a life of unsettled war and his "unhoused free condition/. . . For the sea's worth" (1.2.26–27). Iago, his villainous ensign, maligns him when he describes his discourse as of "a bombast circumstance, / Horribly stuffed with epithets of war" (1.1.13–14). But it is true that his imagery, especially in his most ardent speeches such as the "Farewell" (3.3.345) and his final scene, is dominated by war. His life, even his "perfect soul" (1.2.31), is confined by discipline. When we look beneath the description of mind made tranquil only by battle, we see during the play little knowledge of himself and others. He can win the pitying Desdemona not by ideas but by his physical hardships and his incredible travels. The most moving yet probably the most accurate justification of his tragic folly is that given by himself: he is one "who loved not wisely but too well" (5.2.344). But, as almost always in Shakespeare, we are confronting a miracle. *Othello* painfully moves us as few plays can, in a way that few plays try to do; and despite the fascination of the villain and the gracious charm, pity, and goodness of the heroine, it is Othello himself who transfigures plainness into the wonderful, the mournful, and the beautiful. We can perhaps best appreciate Shakespeare's artistry if we view first what Othello, in another connection, calls his "round [i.e., plain] unvarnished tale" (1.3.90)—here the unpromising outline of the play.

I Will a Round Unvarnished Tale Deliver

In "roundest" terms, *Othello* is a story of raging sexual jealousy prompted apparently by the least credible of motives. Othello has eloped with Desdemona, the white, refined, and pure daughter of a Venetian senator, Brabantio. The Venetian nobility, though not the father, are untroubled by the marriage, a marriage mixed not only by race but also by breeding, gentility, and temperament. The marriage might have succeeded had it not been for one of the most hateful characters ever created: Iago. This essentially puny man is, he tells his dupe Roderigo, jealous because his general Othello has appointed as lieutenant not the seasoned plain veteran Iago but a learned soldier of the new type, Cassio. In soliloquy (1.3.377), Iago tells us also of the reasons for his jealousy and proposed revenge, all of them sexual: he claims both Cassio and Othello have seduced his wife, Emilia, a warm-hearted, simple woman. He proposes, as revenge of wife for wife, to put Othello into such a jealousy as judgment cannot cure. It will take as motive that Desdemona has made the beast with two backs in enjoying the ardors of Cassio.

Because of the nobility of Othello and the transparent purity of

Desdemona, the ruse would seem impossible. But when the action shifts to Cyprus, a town threatened by the Turks, with Othello in command, fortuitous events and Iago's cunning turn Othello from a loving husband who almost worships his wife into a brutal, sadistic, and finally murderously bestial travesty of "the noble Moor." Involved in the stratagem is first a disgraced Cassio who is persuaded to plead to Desdemona for his lost office. When he is so pleading, Othello enters, and Cassio unwisely steals away. This gives Iago the opportunity to cast suspicion on Cassio ("Ha! I like not that," 3.3.35). In "the temptation scene" (3.3) that follows, Iago, with seeming concern for his lord, skillfully instructs the Moor in ways of sexual lust, in what he claims to "think" (3.3.99), and in the loose ways of Venetian women. A major circumstantial aid to him is his wife's discovery of Desdemona's magically wrought handkerchief, an inherited charm of fidelity in love that Othello had given to her. This Emilia gives to Iago, who has it dropped in Cassio's chambers. The handkerchief will, with Iago's help, be thought by Othello to have been given first to Cassio and then to his whore, Bianca. The scene reaches its climax in "sacred" (3.3.461) vows of hatred and revenge by both Othello and Iago, by the latter's promise to kill Cassio, and by Othello's resolve to strangle his lady in her lust-stained bed.

After murdering his wife in a scene mingling ritualistic "justice" (5.2.17), terror, and some eroticism, Othello learns from Emilia how he has been dolted. Venetian officers disarm him and would take him prisoner, but with a final show of nobility, the Moor stabs himself and dies on Desdemona's bed with a final kiss.

A fuller narrative might make the story credibly moving. But one who has not read or seen the play itself would probably still find the story revolting and the character of Othello gullible, cruelly proud, and limited in soul. For Iago, the summary version must, paradoxically, be almost equally regretted, for he provides in the play an almost exhilarating figure of evil.

One must simply conclude that jealousy is a perilous subject for a work of literature as it is for life. It is a narrowing, selfish emotion—almost the opposite of the open heart. And the act of being deceived into jealousy reduces the character to simplemindedness. Shakespeare, however, as we have insisted, courted the perilous. With transfiguring artistry, he makes of jealousy a passion that can shake the noblest of souls, and he makes of the evil beneath it something to cause us to question, as only Shakespeare can, fallible man's responsibility.

We must therefore examine this artistry. Without it the story is too much like what we read in the more lurid papers almost every day. It suggests perverted lust, made ranker by prurient suggestions of sex between races. And such certainly is not the emotional response that all but the safely distanced or meager soul receive from this, the most compact and hard-hitting of Shakespeare's tragedies.

That I Would All My Pilgrimage Dilate

Although not supernatural to the degree that *Hamlet* is, *Othello* descends from a literary genre, the Morality play, that enlarges man's role not to a mere series of events—the round unvarnished tale—but to perhaps the greatest of struggles: that for man's soul. The struggle is of course mainly internal, but these plays were given drama and entertaining value by the almost invariable character of the Vice, a semicomic, mischievous, unconvincingly motivated figure of temptation. The history of this figure has been definitively presented, and applied to *Othello,* by Bernard Spivack.[1] The title of his volume, *Shakespeare and the Allegory of Evil,* is likewise admirably suggestive in helping us lift the play to an imaginative study of evil. Nor is Spivack's theory seriously shaken by an article, Leah Scragg's "Iago—Vice or Devil?,"[2] which claims precedence of the latter character for Iago. True, Othello looks down expecting to find Iago's feet cloven, and in the crucial question of the play he asks: "Will you, I pray, demand that demi-devil / Why he hath thus ensnared my soul and body?" (5.2.301–2). The devil in the Mystery cycles, like the Vice in the Morality play, could be a mischievous tempter of man. But there is no reason that Shakespeare could not have had both traditions in mind. In *Hamlet,* we recall, he successfully draws upon many popular genres, with a resulting complexity and a confusion that have been a source of revenue for scores of scholars, hundreds of critics, and most readers and spectators of the play.

However we may think of Iago, for Othello the Morality play is the more rewarding context and the most persuasive means for enlarging a crude tale of tabloid interest into an allegory both of evil and of mankind. In the first and greatest of the moralities, *Everyman,* the protagonist is "summoned" to a pilgrimage to death. That pilgrimage that Othello will "dilate" (1.3.153) is much broader than the romantic journeys whose narration had won the heart of Desdemona. It is a pilgrimage testing a truer part of his supposedly "perfect soul" (1.2.31) than had the disciplined, physically but not spiritually taxing life of "glorious war." In terms proposed in chapter 1, it will be a testing of a noble warrior in the toils and sophistries of unfamiliar peace, a testing supervised by the foxlike character warned against by Machiavelli. It is, to be sure, a pilgrimage more profound than this. It could befall any man who, in the useful phrase from *King Lear,* "hath ever but slenderly known himself" (1.1.292–93). Nevertheless it is almost individually designed for the Moor. Hamlet, too, goes on a pilgrimage, a vastly different one, and one in which he is also vulnerable in his idealism, but for which, too, he is cunningly equipped by intellect. The difference between the two men and their condign journeys may be the oversimplified possibility that if Hamlet had been the hero of *Othello* or Othello the hero of *Hamlet* there would have been no tragedy. More complex a view is that only Iago could ruin Othello because there is something in Othello that is hospitable to Iago's "poison" (1.1.68). It is something unfamiliar to his experience but not to his aptitude or unconscious evil. It is of course sexual morbidity, but it involves more than sex, even though it surfaces in the potent, lurid vocabulary of pornographic sex. It is, to risk oversimplification again, an inability to accept securely a true and full happiness in love as in life itself.

Othello's character as we first meet him is a somber, though seemingly self-confident one. He has known little happiness in his somewhat distant youth, and the theme of his story to Desdemona is that "of some distressed stroke / That my youth suffered" (1.3.157–58). We should not be surprised by the ill-founded basis he assigns to their marriage: "She loved me for the dangers I had passed, / And I loved her that she did pity them" (1.3.167–8). He is almost consistently afraid of happiness.

This trait is brought out first in the sadness of the story he tells the Senators. It is eloquent also in his attitude toward being dispatched to war on his wedding night: "I do agnize / A natural and prompt alacrity / I find in hardness" (1.3.231–33). It is even more powerfully and sadly expressed in the symbolic, almost supernatural storm prevailing on the sea about Cyprus, described there by a Gentleman: "I never did like molestation view / On the enchafed flood" (2.1.16–17). And the symbolic nature of the tempest is foreseen in Cassio's fears for the safety of his general: "O, let the heavens / Give him defense against the elements, / For I have lost him in a dangerous sea" (2.1.44–46). Cassio will indeed "lose" Othello (and Othello lose Desdemona) on a "dangerous sea." Cassio carries on the motif by his lament: "The great contention of the sea and skies / Parted our fellow-ship" (2.1.92–93).

We are therefore well prepared to read allegory into Othello's emotions upon arriving in Cyprus as he greets his bride:

> O my soul's joy!
> If after every tempest come such calms,
> May the winds blow 'til they have wakened death!
> Or let the laboring bark climb hills of seas
> Olympus-high, and duck again as low
> As hell's from heaven!
>
> (2.1.182–87)

His use of "joy" is, except for a later use in the scene, unique for him—and ultimately troubled:

> If it were now to die,
> 'Twere now to be most happy; for I fear
> My soul hath her content so absolute
> That not another comfort like to this
> Succeeds in unknown fate.
>
> (2.1.187–91)

Further: "I cannot speak enough of this content; / It stops me here; it is too much of joy" (2.1.194–95). His uneasiness with "joy" is more than premonition; it is rooted in his character and former youth. He who knows security only in "hardness" cannot accept more than pity, "content," or "comfort." Consequently, Iago's strategy in the temptation scene is to unsettle whatever glimpses of happiness Othello may have, to play upon his imagined deficiencies and insecurities. Because the marriage is "too much of joy" for Othello to feel confident in, Iago's role is not so brilliant as is usually supposed. It is simply to bring into clearer vision that view of himself and his role in the life that Othello has known well into middle age.

In the context of the theory expressed in chapter 1, our major concern in the temptation scene and what follows is the kind of ordeal Othello experiences and how he confronts it. Once tempted by jealousy, will he succumb to its pornographic vocabulary? Will he escape the torment by hate and by hardening his heart?

We know that, in part, he does all these things. He is "eaten up by passion" (3.3.391). His poetic speech, usually so resonant with his fundamental sadness, takes on the prose accent and imagery of lustily coupling animals of Iago. But never, despite its cunning vividness, does he take pleasure in the pornographic titillation of Iago's language. Unlike much jealousy, his is joylessly free of the masochistic ecstasy others are supposedly enjoying. For him, Iago reflects his own detestation of "the slime / That sticks on filthy deeds" (5.2.149–50).

Othello's language alternately cheapens and grows more beautiful. In this, it reflects his redeeming goodness—to use an uninteresting word rare in modern criticism. Even Iago has to admit that "The Moor is of a free and open nature," a compliment only strengthened by the remainder of the statement, "That thinks men honest that but seem to be so" (1.3.393–94). And the ultimately authoritative Lodovico, once Othello has killed his wife, can only wonder, "O thou Othello that wert once so good" (5.2.291). Basically, Othello is of a "constant, loving, noble nature" (2.1.283). This nature he cannot easily throw off.

His limiting military background is partly responsible for his early reaction to jealousy. He is used to prompt, clear-cut decisions:

> She's gone. I am abused, and my relief
> Must be to loathe her. O curse of marriage,
> That we can call these delicate creatures ours,
> And not their appetite.
>
> (3.3.267–70)

His elementary knowledge of psychology (and of women) is in danger of making him a subject of comedy, even though he never, except in his own eyes, becomes suited to the word *cuckold*.

But later, his growing experience with (not comprehension of) jealousy brings to the surface a capacity for ardent feeling that qualifies him as a Shakespearean hero. When he thinks the suspicion confirmed by Cassio's having his handkerchief, his first emotion is to have Cassio "nine years a-killing" (4.1.175). But then his true ordeal follows hard on: "A fine woman! A fair woman!" (4.1.175–76). Iago reprimands his softness, and again he tries to hate:

> Ay, let her rot, and perish, and be damned
> tonight; for she shall not live. No, my heart
> is turned to stone; I strike it, and it hurts
> my hand.
>
> (4.1.178–81)

The awareness of the hardened heart is ominous, and it should be so for the audience as it is for Othello. But his heart has not irreversibly turned to stone. Love still prevails: "O, the world hath not a sweeter creature! She might lie by an emperor's side and command him tasks" (4.1.181–83). And he continues, praising her skill with a needle, and her music, and her "high and plenteous wit and invention" (4.1.186–87). Later he will at once praise and deplore her physical attractiveness, but now it is not this that holds him to love. Certainly it is his soul, for which he is most to be praised, that prompts his heartbreaking sense of loss: "But yet the pity of it, Iago! / O Iago, the pity of it, Iago!" (4.1.192–93). But within four lines he resolves to "chop her into messes" (4.1.196); and even worse, because it is more sneaking, he changes to a different tactic: "Get me some poison, Iago, this night." (4.1.200).

The pathos of hate and love in combat is repeated with increasing emotional power in two longer scenes. The "brothel scene" (4.2), sadistically cruel because in it he talks to Desdemona as to a whore, is yet full of tearful agony and even ardent tenderness. It redeems him in his wish that heaven were trying him with affliction—a theologically saving belief; and it opens momentarily his heart when he sees his worst affliction—without which he could bear the ordeal—being discarded from "there where I have garnered up my heart" (4.2.57).

The second of these scenes—the terror and the glory of the play—is the murder scene. Like Othello himself, we hate to call a murder what he thinks a sacrifice. Here, Othello—huge, dark, fatal in looks, bearing a torch—bends over the sleeping Desdemona. Upon waking fully, she must ask, as indeed all wives on occasion must ask, "Who is this stranger?" No scene so based is easily conducive to the highest of poetry. Yet, even by itself, it is enough to disprove the earlier suggestion that jealousy is scarcely suited to tragedy. Othello is now the priest, the justice, yes, the sacrificing, erotic husband, who presides over and performs the ritualistic execution, one against which Desdemona can plead only piteously.

We, however, while horrified, are ourselves transfigured by the essential beauty of the "stranger," as Leslie Fiedler calls him. Kissing her repeatedly, he marvels at her beauty: "O balmy breath, that dost almost persuade / Justice to break her sword!" (5.2.16–17). We must almost believe him when he describes his suffering: it is "heavenly; / It strikes where it doth love" (5.2.21–22). Even his later rebuke to Desdemona, that in her refusal to confess "thou dost stone

my heart" (5.2.63), does not alienate him from us. We should probably feel with *his* feeling to his very end, rejecting T. S. Eliot's[3] clever
explanation that Othello, in his final speech, is cheering himself up.

It is better not to look too anxiously into the theology of the outcome. Othello has no doubt that he is damned. But better theologians than he would place more credence and hope in the genuineness
of his final passion. From the stern general who had, as his first line,
the cold " 'Tis better as it is" (1.2.6), he has traversed a pilgrimage
of known and feeling sorrow. And, it must be repeated, it will depend upon the beholder whether one judges or rejoices in the transfig-
uration of loving not wisely but too well.

Chapter Seven
King Lear
Dread Summit

Surely no tragedy, in any language, exceeds the spiritual magnitude of *King Lear*. Testimony to its power and terror, and its almost intolerable grip upon the pity of humanity, is suggested by many criteria. An entire century could not endure the ending with the death of Cordelia. Nahum Tate's debased version, with its happy ending, totally supplanted Shakespeare's tragic rendering of Lear's story so that audiences were scarcely aware that such a rendering existed. Even audiences today, though accustomed to cruelty and terror, are often so overcome by the total experience that—instead of sobbing as for *Romeo and Juliet*—they seem to join in a common exclamation of an almost surprised lament—surprised because they did not realize how much capacity for feeling they had and because they had not known the immensity of the brotherhood they share with their fellows.

Written testimony is also revealing. True, there is much of the usual critical carping over "problems" in the play: for example, the double puzzle of the opening scene, the role of the Fool, and, mainly, outrage at all kinds of injustice in the conclusion, with Lear kneeling beside the body of Cordelia. *Hamlet* has perhaps depended too much for its popularity upon such critical "problems." But the surest guide to the immensity of *King Lear* is to be found not in the relative puniness of what academic critics have to say; the "dread summit" (4.6.57) of the tragedy is better attested to by poets and other literary figures. These are *feeling* responses, close to what an untutored, even unprepared audience endures emotionally.

In these feeling responses there is a remarkable reluctance even to experience the play. It is greatly painful, even too painful. John Keats, in his sonnet "On Sitting Down to Read *King Lear* Once Again," must with reluctance turn away from "golden tongued Romance" on "this wintry day": "Adieu! for, once again, the fierce dispute / Betwixt damnation and impassion'd clay / Must I burn through."[1] Samuel Johnson, though no mean critic and editor, yielded to his true nature as a sensitively moral man when confessing in his "notes": "I was many years ago so shocked by Cordelia's death, that I knew not whether I ever endured to read again the last scenes of the play till I undertook to revise them as an editor."[2]

It was probably not only Charles Lamb's aesthetic reasoning that made him think *Lear* unactable. He could better abide the grander tempest in his own mind, by reading the play. In any case, he pays tribute to the grandeur of the protagonist: "The greatness of Lear is not in corporal dimension, but in intellectual: The explosions of his passion are terrible as a volcano: they are storms turning up and disclosing to the bottom that sea his mind, with all its vast riches." On the stage, Lear depressed Lamb by exposing only "corporal infirmities and weaknesses, the impotence of rage." But on reading the play "we are sustained by a grandeur which baffles the malice of daughters and storms."[3] The danger of this reaction and reasoning—found especially in poets or poetic minds and encouraged by the incomparable verse of the drama—is that *King Lear* becomes not a play but a poem.

Not too many, however, are thus limited. Coleridge, perhaps the best of Shakespearean critics as well as a major poet, comments as only a romantic poet could upon the drama of the mad scene in the hovel (3.4). In doing so, he has found the major way this section can be called "Dread Summit":

All external nature in a storm, all moral nature convulsed,—the real madness ness of Lear, the feigned madness of Edgar, the babbling of the Fool, the desperate fidelity of Kent—surely such a scene was never conceived before or since! Take it but as a picture for the eye only, it is more terrific than any which Michel Angelo, inspired by Dante, could have conceived, and which none but a Michel Angelo could have executed. Or let it have been uttered to the blind, the howlings of nature would seem converted into the role of conscious humanity.[4]

And to take just two more of such tributes by the poetic, we might notice that Swinburne, like Coleridge, and like one of the basic concerns of this study, says that "in this, the most terrible work of human genius . . . , the veil of the temple of our humanity is rent in twain."[5] And William Hazlitt, who like many would prefer not to write about the play at all, yet singles out the assault upon the human heart: "The passion which [Shakespeare] has taken as his subject is that which strikes its roots deepest into the human heart."[6]

The present work takes sustenance from the vital universality of the superlatives by those artisans of the human heart and humanity who have—though with pain—written about *King Lear*. For it is the tragedy that best—perhaps finally—gives voice to what has been admitted to be a persistent hypothesis of this study. No other play is concerned so fully or variously with the testing of the human heart, with the achieving through "known and feeling sorrows" the rescue of threatened humanity. In examining more closely how this testing is dramatically and poetically accomplished, we may well look first at the theme in the play that underlies at once its structure and its challenge: division.

Division

The Renaissance was gifted with a tradition, examined in chapter 1, that would have qualified its audience to understand—without the poetic articulateness of a Coleridge—the underlying source of the play's disturbing power and its tragic challenge. Sir Thomas Elyot and Richard Hooker, among many others, wrote eloquently of the chaos that results when mankind divides. In *Othello* they would have seen in Iago a clever but paltry agent of division. In *King Lear* they would have seen an almost total cast of evil or coldhearted characters who cause and form part of the fractured universe. Not too long before the tragedy, Shakespeare, perhaps influenced most particularly by Hooker, had, in *Troilus and Cressida*, shown and commented upon the dissolution of a state when division takes the form of violated order and degree, the form that inaugurates and persists throughout *King Lear*. Through the keen mind of Ulysses, Shakespeare in *Troilus* states in one of his most powerful philosophical speeches that the heavens and all of nature observe "degree, priority, and place" (1.3.86).

> But when the planets
> In evil mixture to disorder wander
> What plagues, and what portents, what mutiny,
> What raging of the sea, shaking of earth,
> Commotion in the winds, frights, changes, horrors,
> Divert and crack, rend, and deracinate
> The unity and married calm of states
> Quite from their fixture?
>
> (1.3.94–101)

The fundamental division is a violation of "The primogenity and due of birth, / Prerogative of age, crowns, scepters, laurels" (1.3.106–7). The kind of upheaval described and analyzed by Ulysses, even if rhetorically designed, has in its more serious treatment in *King Lear* the same causes; but of course in the later play alone is there such violence of nature attending the loss of prerogative of age and crowns. And only in *King Lear* is there, on a grand scale, more than a political kind of separation.

We must not, however, ignore the political in what is more fully a cosmic depiction of division and dissent. An important, but seldom-read earlier play by Sir Thomas Sackville and Thomas Norton, known usually as *Gorboduc,* may prove useful in showing how the purely political use of division will be instructively dramatized. It is also a possible source for Shakespeare but scarcely so recognized, even though it was important enough to be played, as a warning, before the youthful Queen Elizabeth in 1561.

King Gorboduc, like Lear, decides in his old age to retire and to bestow his kingdom—despite the grave violation of primogeniture—equally between his two sons, Ferrex and Porrex. Like Lear, who would "shake all cares and business" (1.1.39) from his age, he takes comfort in the decision: "In quiet I will pass mine aged days / Free from the travail, and the painful cares, / That hasten age upon the worthiest kings" (1.2.348–50).[7] The state is replete with counselors and flatterers. It has a "parasite" (like Oswald) and a Duke of Cornwall and a Duke of Albany. The wise counselor Philander (meaning "lover of mankind"), an equivalent of Kent, urges Gorboduc not to give up his kingdom:

> And oft it hath been seen, where nature's course
> Hath been perverted in disordered wise,
> When fathers cease to know that they should rule,
> The children cease to know they should obey.
> (*Gorboduc,* 1.2.205–8)

Seeing, like Hooker, the role of nature in unnatural divisions, Philander argues "That Nature has her order and her course, / Which being broken doth corrupt the state / Of minds and things, even in the best of all" (*Gorboduc,* 1.2.220–22). He is pursuing a virtually sacred Elizabethan tenet when he declares: "Within one land, one single rule is best. / Divided reigns do make divided hearts" (*Gorboduc,* 1.2.259–60).

The last line has the most applicability to both *Gorboduc* and *King Lear*. In a considerable sense, both are tragedies of divided hearts. In the early play, both brothers promptly begin to quarrel: the younger

kills the elder (as the younger in *King Lear* would do), and the populace, revulsed by such unnatural doings, mutiny against and kill the
royal pair. Finally, with no head of state, there is universal convulsion, and the play ends without hope, but with a choral warning. For
the student of *King Lear* there is, however, the late role of the
Edmund-like Fergus, who sees in the hapless state a chance to gain
the crown by cunning and force; but nothing comes of this, for the
authors intend mainly to show that a headless state, without an heir,
cannot be reunited. Hence the play lacks an ending. *Gorboduc* is valuable to us principally as a skeletal structure of *King Lear*. It adequately explains the political skeleton racked by division: what *King
Lear* would be without the more skilled weaving of discord with discord, all proceeding from the initial division—Lear's giving up the
crown, dividing his land, disowning Cordelia, and banishing Kent.

To try the impossible—relate coherently the plot of so wide-rang-
ing a play with several stories going on simultaneously—one can do
little more than record sundering after sundering. Lear disowns Cordelia and banishes Kent. The Duke of Burgundy rejects the dowerless
Cordelia. The stonyhearted daughters turn against and turn out the
old man (as they call the king). Meanwhile in the reinforcing subplot
of Gloucester and his sons, the bastard Edmund practices against his
legitimate brother Edgar, convincing the father that Edgar would kill
the aged barrier to preferment; and the brokenhearted, deceived father, Gloucester, thinks that he finds himself in Lear's position. Edgar must flee, disguised as a Bedlam beggar. Lear's two elder
daughters meanwhile, with the vicious Cornwall, turn the blinded
Gloucester from his own home. But they, in turn, separate in lust for
the virile Edmund, Goneril finally poisoning Regan and then killing
herself. Throughout the play, moreover, there are numerous, never
fully exploited references to rumored wars between Albany and Cornwall: division between these two, indeed, is alluded to at the very
beginning of the play. The final and overwhelming separation is that
of the just reunited Lear and his daughter Cordelia. Lear has first
"caught" her, but now, through Edmund's ambitious move against
Albany (Goneril's husband), loses her when Edmund orders her
hanged.

Such may seem, in plot form, to be as much a round, unvarnished
tale—and as inadequate—as that which we essayed for the unfleshed
story of *Othello*. But this is somewhat different, for, although jealousy
pervades more than just the hero of the earlier play, it does not do so
to the extent that separation philosophically pervades *King Lear*.

In his *Laws of Ecclesiastical Polity* (The First Book), besides what we have already noticed in chapter 1 about the convulsion of nature, Richard Hooker speculates about what would happen if the "obedience of creatures unto the law of nature" should fail. So applicable is this to *Lear* that we should remember, and extend, certain of Hooker's words earlier cited:

If the frame of that heavenly arch erected over our heads should loosen and dissolve itself: if celestial spheres should forget their wanted motions, and by irregular volubility turn themselves any way as it might happen . . .; if the moon should wander from her beaten way—

"What would become of man himself, whom these things now do all serve?"[8]

Early in *King Lear,* after the instigating divisions, including the supposed defection of Edgar, Shakespeare devotes two long speeches to the separations in nature, influenced by late eclipses of sun and moon. "Nature," Gloucester tells Edmund,"finds itself scourged by the sequent events" (1.2.103–4). Among the many such enmities he cites are falling off of friendship, mutinies, discord, treason, "the bond crack'd 'twixt son and father; the King falls from the bias of nature, there's father against child" (1.2.106–9). Later, privately, Edmund—a self-reliant skeptic who addresses a mechanistic form of Nature—mocks his father's supposedly superstitious belief in such prophecies. And when Edgar enters, Edmund pretends to be reading from a book on the subject. Though he is mocking, and though in its cheapest form this was judicial astrology concerning which Shakespeare himself may have had doubts, the author of Edmund's book touches the play:

I promise you, the effects he writes of succeed unhappily: as of unnaturalness between the child and the parent; death, dearth, dissolution of ancient amities; division in state, menaces and maledictions against king and nobles; needless diffidences, banishment of friends, dissipation of cohorts, nuptial breaches, and I know not what. (1.2.139–45)

Although (more than in *Romeo and Juliet*) characters outweigh the stars, one should look ahead to the wise and good Kent's appraisal of the discord: "It is the stars, / The stars above us govern our conditions" (4.3.32–33). Moreover, in his allusions to the stars, Shakespeare is following astrology less than the nondeterministic and moral rules of Nature.

Summarizing and pursuing the extent of division in *King Lear*, we should note that not only is there division between Lear and all three of his daughters; between Cordelia and her sisters; between Lear and Kent; between Gloucester and his sons and, later, Gloucester and Cornwall; between Albany and Cornwall; between Edgar and Edmund—besides other lesser enmities. In a still larger, more generalized view, one that could be made to account for virtually all discord in the play, there is division between fathers and children; between king and subjects; between sisters and between brothers; between man and the raging elements; between man and his reason; and, perhaps most important of all, between the good-hearted and the cruel, between the feeling and the unfeeling.

In the next section we shall accompany principally Lear, but also Gloucester, as these two old men, summoned by death, go on their passionate pilgrimage through what Kent calls "this tough world" (5.3.315). We shall keep in mind how both men, each according to his capacity, learn through sorrow what the blinded Gloucester calls seeing feelingly.

Passion and Stature

In an indoor setting, a room of state within Lear's palace, the play begins in a relaxed, even festive mood; for it is to be Lear's ritualistic solemnization of his big decisions: retirement and division. Gloucester, too, appears happily relaxed as he talks with Kent and Edmund about the state and his son's origin and attractiveness. But it is, we must emphasize, an indoor scene, much like the scene of state in *Hamlet,* which was warm with comfort, color, and assurance, following the ominous scene on the outdoor platform.

Nothing but trouble—which will be incongruously huge trouble—will emerge in all directions from this festive opening to *King Lear.* Conversations and ceremony will erupt in all directions into the most violent of passions. First of all, both of the principals, Gloucester and the King, are dangerously self-satisfied. Gloucester talks boastfully in his son's presence about how he had fathered the bastard. "His breeding," he tells Kent, "hath been at my charge. I have so often blushed to acknowledge him that now I am brazed to't" (1.1.8–10). *Brazed* is a dangerous word in Shakespeare; it is akin to the hardened heart and will lead to horrible suffering, explained later by Edgar to Edmund (who agrees):

> The gods are just, and of our pleasant vices
> Make instruments to plague us.
> The dark and vicious place where thee he got
> Cost him his eyes.
>
> (5.3.171–74)

But it is of course Lear's majestic entrance that counts in this great but seemingly simple beginning of the scene. Lear's behavior and Cordelia's response are two of the big "problems" of the play, and as such we should not be overly interested in them. Viewed most probably, the scene is simple, like a folktale, but enriched by Lear's retirement. Retirement is of course what first pleases the King by its generosity and hope of irresponsible comfort. But the audience would be uneasily alerted: kings do not retire. What, however, dominates the scene is the "love contest." The three daughters are to compete in telling their father who loves him most. This is also an act of generosity to the sentimental old man. Its (to us) expected outcome leads to the most repeated cries of passion throughout most of the play: "monster ingratitude" (1.5.34) and "I gave you all" (2.4.245). First it is Cordelia who upsets the ceremony. Later it will be the evil sisters.

Within moments Lear turns in fury upon the youngest, she from whom he had expected most. The change in the scene's tone is sudden and terrifying. Lear of course is from the first an imperial figure of command. Now, and almost to the end, he will be imperious. His outrage against both Cordelia and Kent is the earliest form that passion will take. It is powerful and assured. In the early parts of the play, when Lear is still in self-control, passion conduces to stature. Unlike Gloucester's angry outbursts, which are more querulous, Lear's have terror. But just because his disowning of Cordelia is wrathfully pronounced, we must not neglect the saving quality of intense suffering in it and other oaths. Passion, as we said, meant mainly suffering. Though he curses with fury, it comes from an essentially good heart; and the later curses are essentially sacramental vows. Fundamentally they can be prayers, as when the kneeling ex-King curses Goneril: "Hear, Nature, hear; dear goddess, hear" (1.4.267). Even in wrath Lear learns to feel—first imperiously; then questioningly and uncertainly; then in bizarre madness; then in compassion and humility. His passionate stature is far above that diagnosed at the end of the first scene by Goneril: "the unruly waywardness that infirm and choleric years bring with them" (1.1.297–98).

His cold treatment by Goneril leads to self-questioning. Never having been contradicted by flattering daughters, he begins the journey first toward alienation and then toward self-discovery that will permit him to see himself as a man among other men. His first important questions about his identity are "Does any here know me? This is not Lear" (1.4.216) and the great one—lying latent in us all—"Who is it that can tell me who I am?" (1.4.200). The Fool—in his contrapuntal role as grotesque, fond, enigmatic, disturbing guide to Lear as pilgrim—answers, "Lear's shadow" (1.4.221).

A new manner joins the old imperiousness in the now dwindled authority of Lear. It is a self-dramatization, sometimes clownish, sometimes deeply moving. At this point he cannot command. He responds to Goneril's rebuke with "Your name, fair gentlewoman?" (1.4.226)—only to be humiliated by Goneril's scorn of this and "your other pranks" (1.4.228). Instead of his imperious "Darkness and devils!" (1.4.242) and "Ingratitude! thou marble-hearted fiend, / More hideous when thou show'st thee in a child / Than the sea-monster" (1.4.250–53), he dramatizes querulously his unwillingness to return to Goneril and "Say you have wronged her" (2.4.147). He begins his appeal with "Ask her forgiveness?"

> Do you but mark how this becomes the house:
> "Dear daughter, I confess that I am old.
> Age is unnecessary. On my knees I beg
> That you'll vouchsafe me raiment, bed, and food."
> (2.4.148–51)

His kneeling in dramatizing the incredible act brings a cold comment, "These are unsightly tricks" (2.4.152). So too he will have to wheedle, not irately command, in his plea to retain his hundred knights. He can wheedlingly argue only, "Is this well spoken?" (2.4.231). His stature is reduced, but his passion, as in "O me, my heart, my rising heart" (2.4.116) is taking him closer to poor naked wretches.

He learns self-pity before he learns pity. He dramatizes his plight to the gods. In so doing he stresses his pathetic qualities: "You see me here, you gods, a poor old man, / As full of grief as age, wretched in both" (2.4.267–68). The "answer" Lear receives is the first of many similar stage directions: "Storm and tempest."

In the heath, his passion and his stature go through many changes. He can still piteously challenge the elements for assaulting him: "Here I stand your slave, / A poor, infirm, weak, and despised old man" (3.2.19–20). But he intermittently confronts the tempest with mixed authority and unanswered pathos. A gentleman reports that Lear "Bids the wind blow the earth into the sea" (3.1.5). He "tears his white hair / Which the impetuous blasts, with eyeless rage, / Catch in their fury and make nothing of" (3.1.7–9). In his daughters and mainly in the tempest he has encountered forces less caring than himself.

Nevertheless, he learns in his dwindling, yet never entirely contemptible, commanding passion, to care for the Fool, to respect the broken Edgar ("my philosopher" of grief, 3.4.167), and to ponder on things "would hurt me more" (3.4.25): true need, justice, and, of course, ingratitude. In this learning process toward true feeling, it is testimony to his all-important magnitude as a king ("Ay, every inch a king!," 4.6.106) that even in madness and humility he retains what others see in him, expressed by Kent in one word, "Authority" (1.4.29).

Gloucester, whose suffering fittingly is of the sensual body, becomes a better, more solicitous man. At the risk of his life and the actual loss of his eyes, he helps his King. He never has, however, true stature, and his fall, though hideous, is not so heartrending as Lear's. Lear, towering and essentially alone in his passion, never contemplates suicide. Gloucester folds quickly, and only with Edgar's devoted guidance is saved from despair. Both men are alike in ascending spiritually from hard-hearted complacency. Only Lear remains recognizable as Lear to the very end. His imperial majesty may occasionally bow, but his powerful speech, apparent even in madness by his explosive habit of command, remains even to the imperative "Howl, howl, howl." What happens following this mistaken command to "men of stone" (5.3.257) is of course one of the greatest challenges to the audience in drama.

Tragic Victory of Humanity

And so it will and should remain. Loss of a loved one, particularly of a daughter whom one has wronged, is not in tragedy to be a mere fact of life—as perhaps Lear's death may be rationalized to be. Nor has Shakespeare made the final episode easier for us by comforting language. No episode has more passionately wrenching dramatic poetry or stage action. As human beings, "man's nature cannot," in Kent's earlier words, "carry / Th' affliction nor the fear" (3.2.48–49). We end the play, all passion spent.

Yet Shakespearean tragedy, except for *Timon,* is not pessimistic. Here is the advantage of prefacing the play with some Renaissance knowledge of suffering, through which victorious humanity appears. Lear dominates, yet he is not the whole of the play. And even he is triumphant over the inhuman in a way that will last to the promised end.

The victory of mankind is apparent only if we witness through Lear's (and Gloucester's) "pilgrimage" (5.3.197)—as Edgar calls it—the constant reference to beasts and to a savagery alien to man. Women, notably, are "dog-hearted" (4.3.45), "wolvish" (1.4.299), "tigers not daughters" (4.2.40). Albany charges Goneril, "Bemonster not thy feature" (4.2.63); "Proper deformity seems not in the fiend / So horrid as in woman" (4.2.60–61). A servant, horrified at Gloucester's blinding, says of Regan that if she lives long, "And in the end meet the old course of death, / Women will all turn monsters" (3.7.101–2). Lear feels within himself the taint of having produced "these pelican daughters" (3.4.73). And ingratitude, essentially bestial and a prime mover toward madness, takes the form not only of a fiend but also more terribly of a daughter. It is "More hideous when thou show'st thee in a child / Than the sea-monster" (1.4.251–52).

Lear's most revolting imagining in madness—an imagining important because it leads to his underlying revulsion from sexually animal woman—is his "anatomy" of woman:

> Behold yond simpering dame,
> Whose face between her forks presages snow,
> That minces virtue, and does shake the head
> To hear of pleasure's name.
> The fitchew nor the soiled horse goes to't
> With a more riotous appetite.
> Down from the waist they are Centaurs,
> Though women all above.
>
> (4.6.117–24)

The greatest threat of beast against man, as spoken by Albany to Goneril, has already been noted; but it deserves reemphasis here, for in the total context of the play it presents a challenge to humanity almost as important as that of the last scene:

> If that the heavens do not their visible spirits
> Send quickly down to tame these vile offences,
> It will come,
> Humanity must perforce prey on itself,
> Like monsters of the deep.
>
> (4.2.46–50)

That the threat pervades the play is shown not only in the unnatural daughters. It also appears in Edgar's having "To take the basest and most poorest shape / That ever penury, in contempt of man, / Brought near to beast" (2.3.7–9)—a shape that made his father "think a man a worm" (4.1.33). Critics have questioned why Edgar had to appear begrimed, his hair in knots, and seemingly naked. First one might answer, it *keeps on stage* the basic threat of nakedness, "in contempt of man," bringing him "near to beast." A second reason is that the debased man enabled the mad king to join in the grotesque trio in the hovel, where the cause of madness might appear in his question, "Didst thou give all to thy daughters? And art thou come to this?" (3.4.48–49). More basic still, it led the King to see crazedly (and learningly?) a region of mankind—the bestial—unknown to him in his unphysicked pomp. It made him see, as we are anxious for him to see, man's closeness to the beast:

Is man no more than this? Consider him well. Thou ow'st the worm no silk, the beast no hide, the sheep no wool, the cat no perfume. Ha! here's three on's are sophisticated. Thou art the thing itself; unaccommodated man is no more but such a poor, bare, forked animal as thou art. Off, off, you lendings! (3.4.97–103)

Is Man No More Than This?

The play will affirm that man *is* more than this—that while there are beasts who will blind Gloucester, there is a poor Tom who will lead him. There are servants who will find ointments for his empty sockets. There is also an old retainer, called in Morality tradition (as also in *Doctor Faustus*) simply Old Man, who comes seemingly to help him as he nears death.

And besides Lear's powerful apostrophe to the poor naked wretches in the storm, there is Gloucester's physically sightless comparable view, even in his "huge sorrows" (4.6.276), of these he had neglected when he was "brazed" to lust: "Let the superfluous and lust-dieted man, / That slaves your ordinance, that will not see / Because he does not feel, feel your pow'r quickly" (4.1.67–69). And it is his loyal, abused son who with similar awareness of feeling will describe himself to his father as "A most poor man, made tame to fortune's blows, / Who, by the art of known and feeling sorrows / Am pregnant to good pity" (4.6.217–219).

Too many are there in the play to cite here all the exemplars of humankindness that make man pregnant to good pity. But most compelling are the two who first felt Lear's wrath and unkindness: Kent and Cordelia. These appear appropriately late in episodes that exceed any others Shakespeare would create in showing fellow creatures of feeling humanity. Cordelia's response to the suffering of Lear comes first. Wisely, Shakespeare chose to have it not enacted onstage but—with a quiet pathos more typical of her—related by a Gentleman to Kent. The Earl embodies the audience's most important anxiety, that concerning how the abused daughter will react to letters about Lear's estate. For it is reunion of the two that will be even more meaningful than the chance or old age that will finally lead to their deaths. Cordelia's response is that of a "queen / Over her passion" (4.3.13–14), though "an ample tear trickled down / Her delicate cheek" (4.3.12–13). Kent is insistent to learn that the reunion "moved her" (4.3.15). The Gentleman replies:

> Not to a rage. Patience and sorrow strove
> Who should express her goodliest. You have seen
> Sunshine and rain at once—her smiles and tears
> Were like a better way.
>
> (4.3.16–19)

He further reports

> There she shook
> The holy water from her heavenly eyes,
> And clamor moistened; then away she started
> To deal with grief alone.
>
> (4.3.29–32)

Here her behavior is the closest to Christian doctrine found in the play.

Far different in kind and volume, but not human quality, is the
clamor of the stricken Kent reported in the last scene. Kent's passion
is described by Edgar, the son who, like Kent in mean guise, led the
old man with spiritual safety on his pilgrimage. When, Edgar relates,
Kent discovered "who 'twas that so endured" (5.3.212)

> with his strong arms
> He fastened on my neck, and bellowed out
> As he'd burst heaven, threw him on my father,
> Told the most piteous tale of Lear and him
> That ever ear received; which in recounting
> His grief grew puissant, and the strings of life
> Began to crack.
>
> (5.3.212–18)

So consumed is he, and so devoted, that he will refuse any office in
the kingdom: "I have a journey, sir, shortly to go. / My master calls
me; I must not say no" (5.3.322–23).

During the scene of Lear's death, all eyes in the theater are focused
upon him and the dead Cordelia. This is as it should be. But we must
not overlook the survivors on stage, who form the most important
"audience." It is mainly Lear himself, of course, who serves as "Pre-
senter." He has always had the dramatic sense of most Shakespearean
heroes. And now, in mingled command, reproof, and disbelief, he
superbly directs our emotions toward almost unbearable feeling.

But if Shakespeare's most unwelcome addition to the Lear story was
the death of the King and Cordelia, we must equally credit him with
a profound study in sympathy that redeems man. Albany, Kent, and
Edgar are the onstage presenters who not only enhance the sad spectacle, but also try vainly to rejoin Lear, now losing consciousness or
gaining an ecstasy above consciousness. It is to them that we owe a
choral love that makes of the death scene almost a religious rite:

Kent: Is this the promised end?

Edgar: Or image of that horror?

Albany: Fall and cease. (5.3.264–65)

                        . . .

Kent: Break, heart, I prithee break!

Edgar: Look up, my Lord.

Kent: Vex not his ghost. O, let him pass! He hates him
          That would upon the rack of this tough world
          Stretch him out longer. (5.3.313–16)

The play had begun in division. Humanity had preyed upon itself. But, despite terrible loss, it ends in union; a union that is worth more, though more dearly bought, than a "happy" ending. Without this tragic victory of the poor, small, wounded band—and not least the final settlement of the state—there might be an easy comfort but not an exhausting exultation.

Chapter Eight
Macbeth

Vaulting Ambition: Full with Horrors

Within scarcely a year of *King Lear,* Shakespeare produced another masterpiece. If we add *Hamlet* and *Othello, Macbeth* concludes the quartet of tragedies generally recognized as an unparalleled achievement. They are like one another in power, passion, and poetry; yet the individual achievement of each is as remarkable as their invariable grandeur.

Macbeth stands especially apart because here the hero becomes progressively evil. And not only he. With his wife, we take another major step in Shakespeare's career. Gertrude had been a complex woman, older than her predecessors and a mixture of queenliness, motherhood, and immorality. The evil sisters in *King Lear* are also older, more cunning in worldly ways, and more heartless than any (except for the inhuman Tamora) before them. Lady Macbeth, however, is one of a majestic trio of women in his later tragedies, followed in her major role by Cleopatra and by Volumnia in *Coriolanus.* The result is to be seen in the fuller dimensions of life in these plays. We can no longer conveniently speak of "the protagonist," though we must do so in *Macbeth,* for although his lady for a time dominates him, and although her tragedy is almost equal to his, he dominates the play. But for the first time (at least since the child Juliet) we can welcome more than a male hero into the sorrow and glory of tragedy.

Led by prophecies of the Weird Sisters, by "vaulting ambition" (1.7.27), and by the "valor" (1.5.25) of his Lady's tongue, the fierce and loyal general Macbeth—again like earlier heroes—reluctantly takes on a mission alien to his deepest nature: the murder of the king, "gracious Duncan" (3.1.66). For barely the first act are husband and wife together in spirit, first in the excitement of the "deed" (2.2.14) and then in unexpected profusion of blood. Lady Macbeth overcomes for only a while the moral scruples and terrible visions of her husband: "A little water clears us of this deed" (2.2.66); "how easy is it then" (2.2.67); "leave all the rest to me" (1.5.71). Regicide is terrible, and all of Scotland is convulsed on the "unruly" (2.3.50) starless night of Duncan's murder. When the dead king is discovered in the morning in Macbeth's castle where he had been a guest, the loyal thanes, ultimately suspecting the murderer, unite in horror, but Macbeth becomes king. Banquo, a tempted but loyal thane, serves as foil to Macbeth. Macduff flees to England for military aid against the "tyrant, bloody sceptered" (4.3.104). But Banquo, who according to the Weird Sisters is "not so happy yet much happier" (1.3.66) because he will "get kings though [thou] be none" (1.3.67), is cut down by murderers suborned by Macbeth, who has become victim to paranoid fears. Consequently, when Banquo obligingly appears at Macbeth's banquet, he appears as a ghost, with twenty mortal gashes on his head, taking the chair before the tyrant. For one of Macbeth's punishments is that he can no longer be a part of humanity or break bread with his fellow man. "The table's full" (3.4.46). Driven still compulsively, Macbeth has Macduff's entire family slaughtered. Malcolm and Macduff succeed in leading an army from England and killing Macbeth. The Queen who, like her husband, has known not a single moment of joy since Duncan's murder, goes mad, walks nightly in her sleep, and kills herself. The state, under the new reign of Duncan's rightful heir, Malcolm, is now "free" (5.8.55)—free from murderers and bloody banquets. And free from the horrors that raged within Macbeth's now severed head—horrors that had made of him more than the "dead butcher" (5.8.69) he is finally called.

Of a brave warrior who has been a loyal, trusted subject and kinsman, we can only ask why he did the murder. We wonder equally why Shakespeare would choose a man so eminently unsuited for murder to do it. He was awesomely fierce in warfare, "unseaming" (1.2.122) the "merciless Macdonwald" (1.2.9) "from the nave to th' chops" (1.2.22). But, as often with warriors, he is unsuited to do meaner crimes. His wife says of him, when she receives his letter telling of the thrilling prophecy: "Yet do I fear thy nature, / It is too full o'th' milk of human kindness / To catch the nearest way" (1.5.14–16).

Another disability for heinous crime is his vulnerability to visions, to the imagination. He can face the brutal realities of battle but not the ghastly human extensions: "Present fears / Are less than horrible imaginings" (1.3.137–38). It is possible that, just as he speaks some of the most terrifying and sadly beautiful poetry in Shakespeare, so he may be beneath his "rugged" (3.2.27) exterior a sensitive seer.

What is at once his curse and his virtue, therefore, is that he must picture the murder before he does it. Not merely his eyes are affected. Only a man who *feels* can transmute prosaic fear into "I have supp'd full with horrors" (5.5.13).

Shakespeare has achieved one of the most thrilling and painful of murder stories through what might be considered a cruel trick on us. Most such stories are seen from the safe outside. We are innocent spectators who have the coolly complacent role of trying to find, and punish, the criminal. As Thomas De Quincey, that connoisseur of the art, saw, in murder, the victim is a vulgar creature.[1] The interest, though not the sympathy, must be placed within the murderer. Hence, as almost alone except for *Crime and Punishment*, we live through the temptation, the crime, and the terrible guilt through the eyes of Macbeth. It is, one trusts, our one opportunity to experience the act of murder.

This is of course not only a frightening inversion for us: we, if honest, must admit that we are at first on Macbeth's side, though revolted at what he does. Especially important, the play tests us—our sensibilities, our ambition, our manhood, our closeness to our wife, and the contrasting strength of our loyalty to a king. In this play, perhaps more than in any other, we must face with a murderer a moral choice.

Fair Is Foul, and Foul Is Fair

With the line "Fair is foul, and foul is fair" in the first scene from that chant by the Weird Sisters (only in speech headings are they called witches), we are introduced to the apparent moral ambiguity of the play and also to the extremely important supernatural. L. C. Knights has called attention to "the reversal of values"[2] in *Macbeth*, but the implication of the line can be carried much further.

To speak first of linguistic matters, "fair" and "foul" often go together, and the result is confusing, but sometimes clarifying and enriching in meaning. Macbeth's first line in the play is "So foul and fair a day I have not seen" (1.3.38). In several ways this is true. The day is stormy; Macbeth and Banquo have won a major victory; in a sense Macbeth will soon know, he will be hailed Thane of Cawdor and "King hereafter"; and, with a final irony (in which the play is so taut), the day will be most foul for him in body and soul. So persuasive and consistent are the uses of these words, that whenever we encounter "fair" we also should read "foul." After Macbeth receives the prophecy, Banquo comments upon his "partner's" strange behavior: "Good sir, why do you start and seem to fear / Things that do sound so fair?" (1.3.51). These lines not only should alert us to the ironic potential of the "fair" for Macbeth; they may also be a clue that Macbeth is not altogether innocent of what the prophecy entails. One final example of the fair-foul linkage may be cited. When Duncan visits Macbeth's castle at Inverness, his greeting is enough to cast as much dark doubt upon the Lady as the previous lines do upon Macbeth. Duncan's lines are as pure and gracious as the recipient is foul: "Fair and noble hostess, / We are your guest tonight" (1.6.24–25).

There are other kinds of sinister ambiguities or double meanings that confound the moral issues. They do so mainly for Macbeth, of course; for though he has premonitions, we have the advantage of sensing more than he. In short, he is the victim of irony.

He is primarily the victim of those masterly purveyors of irony, the Weird Sisters. He is baffled by their promises, foul and fair: "This supernatural soliciting / Cannot be ill, cannot be good" (1.3.130–31). Later he speaks bitterly of their mischievous tricks that have contributed to his ruin:

> And be these juggling fiends no more believed
> That palter with us in a double sense,
> That keep the word of promise to our ear
> And break it to our hope.
>
> (5.8.19–20)

When they are discussing the prophecy, and Macbeth betrays his excitement, the more wary Banquo cautions him concerning the only seeming fairness of those creatures:

> But 'tis strange:
> And often times, to win us to our harm,
> The instruments of darkness tell us truths,
> Win us with honest trifles, to betray's
> In deepest consequence.
>
> (1.3.122–26)

But for Macbeth, the "honest trifles" are understandably compelling. They are "two truths" serving "as happy prologues to the swelling act / Of the imperial theme" (1.3.127–29). We must not—we who also in a sense are "partners"—too easily dismiss his moral predicament.

What we should, with Banquo, know is that "these" (1.3.39)—as Banquo first calls the Sisters—are more than witches who can tend a cauldron, make charms, and chant. They are more than filthy old women, with beards, more than "secret, black, and midnight hags" (4.1.48). For witches are merely, in Elizabethan demonology, pledged servants to Satan, who is seeking man's "eternal jewel" (3.1.68). The forces of evil behind the witches are what Banquo calls "the instruments of darkness" (1.3.124). They can prophesy, but they can also seduce. As witches they can "poison," but only if there are willing victims.

In the search for Macbeth and his lady as victims, the weird sisters encounter also the tempted Banquo, foil to Macbeth. Shakespeare effectively uses him to show that succumbing to the instruments of darkness is not inevitable. And to confirm the point, he must characterize Banquo as, like Macbeth, sorely tempted. On a lesser scale than in *King Lear* there is a double plot. Two noble men, at the crest of their careers, are told—with supporting evidence—of great futures. Some tainted action seems necessary in each case. Only Banquo, not without a grim struggle, will keep, as he tells Macbeth, "My bosom franchised and allegiance clear" (2.1.28).

True, in his comparable pilgrimage, Banquo does not undergo the mysterious emotions of his partner. Macbeth in anguish asks himself why he is confronted by two equally foul and fair auguries:

> If good, why do I yield to that suggestion·
> Whose horrid image doth unfix my hair
> And make my seated heart knock at my ribs
> Against the use of nature?
>
> (1.3.134–37)

But Banquo, without equal agitation, must fight off the evil that the demonic powers have concentrated upon both men, and he does so in a scene appropriately clothed in troubling night. It is meaningfully a scene that begins the second act, the scene of Macbeth's murder of Duncan. The first line is a question Banquo asks his son Fleance: "How goes the night, boy?" (2.1.1). The answer, as in *Hamlet* with the ghost, is midnight. Banquo cannot—or rather would not—sleep:

> A heavy summons lies like lead upon me,
> And yet I would not sleep. Merciful powers,
> Restrain in me the cursed thoughts that nature
> Gives way to in repose.
>
> (2.1.6–9)

Banquo had dreamed last night of the three Weird Sisters, and it is partly that and partly the fear of the "cursed thoughts" that excite his apprehension. Nicholas Remy, in his *Demonaltry,* had written:

Therefore they bring that misfortune upon themselves, who give themselves to sleep without having first prayed and besought Almighty God for His help; since . . . that is their safest shield and protection against all the wiles of the Prince of Darkness. But the minds of men who are about to sleep too often wander into evil imaginings.[3]

Shakespeare had a limited but essential and accurate knowledge of theology. He correctly recognized, as Walter Clyde Curry notes,[4] that the "Powers" to whom Banquo prays are the order of angels appointed by God to guard against demons. The compelling question in the first and crucial part of the play is whether Macbeth will battle against the most deadly of enemies. And it is in this first part, in act 1, that in his reaction to "supernatural soliciting" (1.3.130) he reveals the most appealing part of the "feeling sorrow" that he can so beautifully express.

I Am Settled

Much has been written supporting the thesis that Macbeth is a hapless victim of fate, and certainly a superficial (yet sensitive) reading of the play makes us feel that destiny here is as strong as in *Romeo and Juliet* and *Julius Caesar*. Evidence is nevertheless strong and ultimately attractive that a man of Macbeth's moral sensibility has a moral choice. Admittedly his Lady has a compelling influence upon him. And this power will be "fiendlike" (5.8.69) as well as human.

But even before they meet after news of the prophecy, he has, as we noted, been startled and fearful upon hearing it. On his own, moreover, he has virtually conjured evil after hearing that Malcolm is named Prince of Cumberland. His aside has what will become his habitual accent, a style solemn in ritual:

> Stars, hide your fires;
> Let not night see my black and deep desires.
> The eye wink at the hand; yet let that be
> Which the eye fears, when it is done, to see.
> (1.4.50–53)

The speech is also characteristically at Macbeth's expense ironic. He asks for, and is granted in a juggling sense, a kind of moral anaesthesia. He will not see now, for fear, yet he will after "it is done" *see*. And the horrid sights will be a major part of his later "torture of the mind" (3.2.21).

We must also take into vigilant account the first appearance of the Sisters. In their chanting song they ask when they shall meet again. It will be "When the battle's lost and won"; it will be "in thunder, lightning, and in rain" upon the heath. Most important in the plans is the line "There to meet with Macbeth" (1.1.1–7). There may, to be sure, be ironic prophecy about Macbeth in the battle that, for them, is both "lost and won" (1.1.4). They know of him that fair is foul. But why do they so readily identify Macbeth as the subject of their meeting? Have they randomly chosen a victim who is only seemingly fair? We need rather recognize what Elizabethans knew: that demons seek out an important man because he has in some way solicited them. Almost all theatergoers would have known that Mephistophilis comes to Doctor Faustus because he has been summoned. And that Macbeth had earlier contemplated complicity is probable from what Lady Macbeth reminds her husband when he falters: "What beast was't then / That made you break this enterprise to me?" (1.7.47–48).

Before Macbeth yields primacy to the Sisters, and even afterward, he goes through one of the most memorable internal struggles Shakespeare ever wrote. Murder, we have suggested, is not congenial to Macbeth. Beyond this, however, is a fair nature that abhors regicide. He may feebly explain to his Lady, in practical terms she might grasp, that he has won "golden opinions" (1.7.33) that he would enjoy. But privately he reveals, besides his fear of "the life to come" (1.7.7), that powerful Elizabethan passion: conscience. It works more strongly in him, and in far more poignant poetry, than in Claudius as he attempts to pray. Here we can look briefly only at his most characteristic soliloquy of regret, the famous "If it were done when 'tis done" (1.7.1). Proceeding in it from fear of "Bloody instructions, which, being taught, return / To plague th'inventor" (1.7.9–10), he moves to a more sorrowful feeling: pity and horror at killing the virtuous Duncan. Even more to Macbeth's credit in this outcry is that it occurs after he has committed himself to the deed. Macbeth, with a still not dead moral sensitivity, deeply feels how evil it is to kill a man "here in double trust" (1.7.10). Then comes the most heartfelt agony of the soliloquy, aglow with imagery the likes of which Shakespeare had never essayed before:

> Besides, this Duncan
> Hath borne his faculties so meek, hath been
> So clear in his great office, that his virtues
> Will plead like angels, trumpet-tongued against
> The deep damnation of his taking-off,
> And pity, like a naked new-born babe
> Striding the blast, or heaven's cherubin horsed
> Upon the sightless couriers of the air,
> Shall blow the horrid deed in every eye
> That tears shall drown the wind.
>
> (1.7.16–25)

The images are not yet those of a tale told by an idiot, full of sound and fury. They come from the heated imagination and the wounded heart. And the heart, as characteristically in *King Lear,* is bleeding for someone else. If Macbeth had been able to maintain this intensity of feeling, in which new-born babes stride the blast and tears drown the wind, he would not only have "lived a blessed time" (2.3.88), but also have taken a rightful place among those of Shakespeare's heroes who are redeemed by sorrow.

But, in perhaps his most crucial speech, he commits himself to Satan. Finally acceding to his Lady's pressure, he promises sadly and wearily: "I am settled, and bend up / Each corporal agent to this terrible feat" (1.7.79–80). Even closely attentive scholars have missed the impact of those lines. Based upon well-known biblical doctrine, they spell his doom and his inevitable future downward to despair and dusty death. They are his words of moral choice. The biblical reference is Romans 6:13–16:

13 Neither yield ye your members as instruments of unrighteousness unto sin: but yield yourselves unto God, as those that are alive from the dead, and your members as instruments of righteousness unto God. . . .

16 Know ye not, that to whom ye yield yourselves servants to obey, his servants ye are to whom ye obey; whether of sin unto death, or of obedience
unto righteousness?

By thus committing his members to Satan (as he could do only more
luridly, like Faustus, if he were to write in blood), Macbeth becomes
King. But the "settled" is deeply ironic, for he will be more driven
in restless ecstasy to seek final security. This will require endless
crime, but the killing of Banquo is most important, for in resolving
upon it, he expresses his own great loss:

> For Banquo's issue have I filed my mind;
> For them the gracious Duncan have I murdered;
> Put rancors in the vessel of my peace
> Only for them, and mine eternal jewel
> Given to the common enemy of man
> To make them kings—the seeds of Banquo kings.
>   (3.1.65–70)

And the bending up of his members will further lead to the terrible
"fits" (3.4.21) that will torment him until he has lost one of his most
saving features, his moral imagination.

Consider It Not So Deeply

So close—especially before their lonely moments after the murder—are Macbeth and his "dearest partner of greatness" (1.5.10–11)
that one could tell a large part of their tragedy from her point of
view. Yet her view would be different in attitude toward the murder
and much more pathetic afterward. She has lived only for her husband. Her most poignant cry during the murder scene is "My husband!" (2.2.12). The sad irony is that though in one speech she
correctly assesses Macbeth's milk of human kindness and the illness
that should attend it, for the most part she fails to understand his
moral struggles, his poetic tendencies, his daggers of the mind, his
horror at blood, and finally the Frankenstein monster that she has set
in motion.

Before the murder, she is magnificent in control and resolution.
She scarcely has heard that "the King comes here tonight" (1.5.29)
before she consecrates herself, in one of the most dreadful speeches of
the play, to "you spirits / That tend on mortal thoughts" (1.5.38–

39) and to "you murd'ring ministers, / Wherever in your sightless substances / You wait on nature's mischief" (1.5.46–48). What is lacking in her conjuration is Macbeth's poetic incantation. He is, of course, prosaic in "Each corporal agent" (1.7.80), but she is much more factually specific in her mention of being unsexed. Only in the conclusion of her "prayer," and almost no place else in the major part of the play, does she achieve a fraction of his verbal music:

> Come, thick night,
> And pall thee in the dunnest smoke of hell,
> That my keen knife see not the wound it makes,
> Nor heaven peek through the blanket of the dark
> To cry "Hold, hold!"
>
> (1.5.48–52)

In her early domination she is cruel even in imagery. Instead of "Pity, like a new-born babe striding the blast," she expresses her fierce resolve by a willingness to pluck a sucking baby from her bosom and dash the brains out. She taunts her hesitating, but admiring, husband with fierce flickings of insult. She uses, but with unique cutting force, the three time-honored humiliations visited by woman upon man: you promised me; you are not a man; and you do not love me. In response, he can cry only—revealing a potential to remain full of humanity—"Prithee peace! / I dare do all that may become a man / Who dares do more is none" (1.7.46–48). And the vicious quality of her argument is shown in the already quoted reply: "What beast was't then / That made you break this enterprise to me?" Macbeth knows his wife's steely determination, her practical, prosaic temperament. To give his deepest reasons to her would be futile. So he weakly replies, "If we should fail?" (1.7.59). A world of moral sensitivity remains unspoken. When therefore she directs him, "We fail? / But screw your courage to the sticking place / And we'll not fail" (1.7.59–61), he comes as close to her in spirit as he will ever do again: "Bring forth men-children only / For thy undaunted mettle should compose / Nothing but males" (1.7.72–74).

From all of this, one might suppose that she lacks the female equivalent of the manliness she fails to find in Macbeth: womanliness. Assuredly during the murder it is she who must direct him, she who must return the bloody daggers to the chamber and smear the grooms.

But to fail to see her womanliness would be to fail to see her great ambition for her husband, to ignore her surprising "Had he not resembled / My father as he slept, I had done't" (2.2.12–13), to over-look her horrified passion during the murder and what follows, and finally, to disregard the probable genuineness of her fainting.

Her story of the tragedy from now on could be put together from the nightmarish fragments of her magnificent sleepwalking scene. For it is there that her horror of this and subsequent murders—now kept under perhaps hysterical control—surfaces from the unconscious. It is there that we hear of the "damned spot" (5.1.32), the hand washing, the smell of blood, her continual need for light by her, and her inti-mation of the fate confronting both criminals: "Hell is murky" (5.1.33). But while these betray the hidden frailty of womanhood, we should not ignore her concern for her husband that—we did not know well enough—absorbed her during the murder. For though the filthiness of the blood most disturbs her surprising daintiness as a woman, that which most haunts her is reliving what had been her all-consuming anxiety during the scene: directing and controlling her strangely behaving husband. She once more hopelessly tries to reas-sure him, for to her "Th'attempt, and not the deed / Confounds us" (2.2.10–11). She taunts the now forever separated husband: "Fie, my lord, fie! a soldier and afeard? What / need we fear who knows it, when none can call our / power to accompt?" (5.1.33–35). But she herself immediately proceeds to vent her own heartsickness: "Yet who would have thought the old man to have had so much blood in him?" (5.1.35–37). She reverts, however, to her task: "No more o'that, my lord, no more o'that! You mar all with this starting" (5.1.40–42). She urges him as in the actual murder scene, to put on his night-gown: "To bed, to bed! There's knocking at the gate" (5.1.61). And in a surprisingly moving gesture, she tries to regain her long-es-tranged husband. Recalling their one-time conjugal life, she asks to take his hand. Her last words as she seeks him are, "To bed, to bed, to bed!" (5.1.63).

That these two evil, yet not totally evil, creatures are essentially and ultimately separate can best be gleaned, however, only from her failure to understand him during the murder scene. Perhaps a part of her ignorance is a steel will despising the weakness that fears bloody sights and hears voices. But her prosaic mind is a sufficient barrier to his imaginative one. It is she who arranges systematically all the equipment of the murder and drugs the grooms. For her, failure of the deed is failure enough. For him, on the other hand, the evil of the deed is all. He feels none of her expected rejoicing in her tense, expectant, and sinister "He is about it" (2.2.4). She cannot understand the sadness of his prose line made somehow poetic: "I have done the deed" (2.2.14). When, however, he looks at his bloody hands and observes, "This is a sorry sight" (2.2.20), there may be, besides anger, a hysterical foreshadowing of her sleepwalking in her scolding remark, "A foolish thought, to say a sorry sight" (2.2.21). What, as a committed fiend, she cannot grasp is his horror at being unable to say "Amen" (2.2.28) when one of the grooms said "God bless us" (2.2.29). There is surely mounting fright in her advice, "Consider it not so deeply" (2.22.29). And there is an unmistakable panic of approaching madness in her cry, when he persists in his "need of blessing" and need to say "Amen" (2.2.31). She may be morally obtuse, but she is partly in the fearful murkiness of hell when she protests: "These deeds must not be thought / After these ways; so it will make us mad" (2.2.32–33). Finally, only the sleepwalking scene will betray what she does comprehend from her husband's "multitudinous seas incarnadine" (2.2.61) lament. The irony of this partial comprehension only underscores her essential aloneness: "A little water clears us of this deed. / How easy is it then!" (2.2.66–67). Guilt implacably separates.

Whence Is That Knocking?

The Porter's scene—"On the Knocking at the Gate in *Macbeth*," as De Quincey calls it—would before this rehabilitating essay have seemed indecorous as the conclusion to this chapter. But the scene is a great one, both for its once-despised raucous humor and for its presentiment of the return of a normal world.

The present success of the episode of the drunken porter may seem incongruous even today. Its topical humor, its reference to the "equivocator" (2.3.8) and to the "farmer which hanged himself on th'expectation of plenty," (2.3.4–5), is unfunny today. Seemingly all that delights audiences is the lurching gait and the slurred speech of the clown and the mildly humorous "Knock, knock, knock" (2.3.3). The miracle is the almost hysterical laughter with which today's audiences respond to what they cannot understand. The explanation is simply a tribute to Shakespeare's sense of theatrical necessity. Readers do not laugh at the Porter. The episode concludes the scene of the darkest, most horrible murder in Shakespeare. The audience, not only suffering from the blood, also suffers involuntarily, as De Quincey shows, with the murderers. Shakespeare knew that audiences can stand only so much horror without meaningless hysterical laughter. He accordingly—as in *Romeo and Juliet*—provided for the release of tension, keeping emotional control in his own hands.

The knocking also deserves appreciative analysis. Nothing is more frightening than loud knocking at night, especially to guilty, fearful souls. We share in their apprehension. But the principal victim is the man with "pestered senses" (5.2.23)—senses agitated by a consecration of "each corporal agent" (1.7.80) to Satan: "Whence is that knocking? / How is't with me when every noise appals me? / What hands are here? / Ha! they pluck out mine eyes" (2.2.56–58). For not only sounds but also sights will affright him, and he will later cry, "But no more sights!" (4.1.155).

In a deeper sense, however, the scene is at Hell-Gate, and appropriately the drunken porter takes the role of gatekeeper. The scene is very close, even in the role of the porter as the character Rybald, to the playlet within the Miracle Cycles depicting "The Harrowing of Hell." Glynne Wickham has pointed to parallels that place the scene in hell:

On the medieval stage hell was represented as a castle, more particularly as a dungeon or cesspit within a castle. . . . Its gate was guarded by a janitor or porter. Christ, after his crucifiction, but before his resurrection, came to this castle of hell to demand of Lucifer the release of the souls of the patriarchs and prophets. The setting for this play was either the interior of the gate-house or the courtyard of the castle: Christ's arrival was signaled by a tremendous knocking at this gate and a blast of trumpets.

Moreover, "thunder, cacophony, screams, and groans were the audible emblem of Lucifer and hell on the medieval stage."[5]

The "alarum bell" (2.3.70) and the awakening of the sleepers by Macduff foreshadow the coming of daylight in a story of the night. Macduff's truly manly voice calling "murder" (2.3.70) brings into the open for the first time the crime muffled entirely by darkened words of Macbeth and his Lady. It is not "murder"; it is "the night's great business" (1.5.66) (*business* is borrowed four times by the husband), "enterprise" (1.7.48), and especially "deed" (1.7.14), a witches' word.

The "awful parenthesis" in nature, as De Quincey calls the murder scene,[6] is to be over. "The night," Malcolm predicts, "is long that never finds the day" (4.3.240). And "The time is free" (5.8.55), Macduff pronounces after he has slain the "tyrant" (4.3.12). What this connotes is eloquently voiced by a Lord:

> We may again
> Give to our tables meat, sleep to our nights,
> Free from our feasts and banquets bloody knives,
> Do faithful homage and receive free honors—
> All which we pine for now.
>
> (3.6.33–37)

The "awful parenthesis" produces sadness of great beauty. And even as the forces of liberation advance upon Scotland, we are still "rapt" (1.3.57), almost hypnotized, with Macbeth in his disenchanted speeches of loss. We may in our confused state of mingled rapture and relief recall George Meredith's "Lucifer in Starlight," a poem about that great dark figure who meteorically rose, but only in a moral universe around whom "marched rank on rank / The army of unalterable law."[7]

Chapter Nine
Timon of Athens

Admiration and Bafflement:
Approaches to an Unusual Tragedy

If one finds pleasure in Shakespeare's plays mainly in their "problems," one could do worse than to give days and nights to the study of *Timon*. It has the special advantage of being questionable as a total play: its date, its genre, its degree of "completeness," and the certain authorship of some parts. But the play also has virtues and interests more literary. Almost surely Shakespeare (and Shakespeare alone) wrote it during his later period of great tragedies, emphasizing themes with which he was then absorbed. It has in the last two acts poetry of passionate power, resembling and even rivaling, as in its theme of ingratitude, *King Lear,* which it probably shortly followed.

It is, take it all in all, an imperfect yet formidable play. Coleridge called it "an after vibration" of *King Lear*.[1] G. Wilson Knight, in an essay titled informatively "The Pilgrimage of Hate," considered the play "archetypal" in its theme and one that is "conceived on a scale even more tremendous than that of *Macbeth* and *King Lear*; and whose universal tragic significance is of all most clearly apparent." Unlike most critics, he wisely chooses "to concentrate on whatever is of positive power and significance."[2] Even critics who do not greatly enjoy the play, or would avoid Knight's enthusiasm, are wary enough to respect the play (it is perilous to undervalue Shakespeare), as they have done with a comparably imperfect masterwork, *Troilus and Cressida*.

Nevertheless, few Shakespearean students, however conscientious and wary, honestly like the entire play. Keats did not write a sonnet "On Sitting Down to Read *Timon* Once Again." And even conscientious Shakespeareans somehow fail to reread the play, which has proved equally unsuccessful in attracting performances. Those who even *know* the play tend to return to it only when in a bilious condition. It is a mirror for those of us who are sick of man's ingratitude or nauseously disenchanted by mankind itself. No other play, not even *Troilus* with its Thersites, provides so satisfying a vocabulary of virulent bitterness. It is a play of an intemperance not easily associated with the "free" and godlike dramatist. And of special worry to the present study, it depicts a protagonist unattractively worsening during his ordeal, falling more precipitously than Macbeth, and, for at least two acts, railing against the Renaissance ideal of man.

It is customary for the wary critics of Shakespeare to explain away anomalies like these. The play, accordingly, has been interpreted not as a conventional tragedy. It can be understood, as in the latest (and perhaps only) substantial book on the play, as a tragedy of pessimism.[3] But this placement requires a learned justification of a Shakespearean pessimistic tragedy—one that leaves the viewer without the usual sense of uplifting fulfillment. Rolf Soellner, the author, seeks—and possibly finds—the justification in Schopenhauer rather than in Aristotle or the Elizabethans. *Timon* has also been seen in the category of "tragical satire" (by O. J. Campbell)[4] or as "spectacular" drama (by J. M. Nosworthy).[5] Finally, and most satisfactorily, it has been placed on "Shakespeare's tragic frontier," the world of his final tragedies, in which the paradoxical temper of the Jacobean period conduced to a mixture of "taints" and "honors" in the hero, and led to a deeply flawed nobility, beyond which tragedy could not go while remaining tragedy. It is a world far different from the earlier period highlighted by *Hamlet.* This theory, presented in a learned, judicious book by Willard Farnham,[6] is useful to the view taken by the present chapter. It is especially useful, if perhaps too uniform, for us as we proceed from *Timon* to *Antony and Cleopatra* and *Coriolanus.* But while it makes incontrovertible use of the mood of the times, it requires closer appreciation of the genre of the play and, even more so, of the play considered in its own, often self-formulated terms.

Much of the bafflement felt by critics has been with the matter of "completeness." If, as is usually now recognized, Shakespeare is responsible for the entire play, the many confusions of verse and prose, the manifest inconsistencies, and other unlucky peculiarities (extending even to vast discrepancies in value of a talent) must be somehow accounted for. There is, for example, a "ghost" figure called simply Mercer, who has no part in the play but presumably was to have one. Poet and Painter actually appear long after their announced entrance in act 5. And Timon has not one but two contradictory epitaphs. These and many other "problems" are now explained as marks of a play that Shakespeare did not complete.

The present chapter questions, as have few other works, what "completeness" means. It more confidently than other works affirms that the total play is complete in that it fulfills Shakespeare's design. It looks upon the presumed flaws as scarcely more important than imperfect proofreading. Most important, by looking intently at the format of the play, it affirms not fundamental "errors" of construction but rather a tragedy designed with unusual, even excessive, care. If the play is not popular, it is not mainly because it is unpleasant, or roughly crafted, but because it is insistent and sometimes monotonous in hammering home a message. The case for a dominating moral message rests upon a didactic introductory statement of theme; upon many flimsy, obvious, often abstract characters; upon an unwelcome proportion of talking; and upon a structure so formal that it seems intended for a moral play rather than for a variously paced drama with surprises.

Moral Painting

Poet and Painter at the very beginning of the play are given speeches in Timon's home moralizing upon their noble host. Poet in particular, at a length unlikely to hold an audience, tells of a poem he is prepared to present to Lord Timon. He begins:

> You see this confluence, this flood of visitors:
> I have in this rough work shaped out a man
> Whom this beneath world doth embrace and hug
> With amplest entertainment.
>
> (1.1.42–45)
>
> . . .
>
> You see how all conditions, how all minds,
> As well of glib and slipp'ry creatures as
> Of grave and austere quality, tender down
> Their services to Lord Timon. His large fortune,
> Upon his good and gracious nature hanging,
> Subdues and properties to his love and tendance
> All sorts of hearts; yea, from the glass-faced flatterer
> To Apemantus, that few things love better
> Than to abhor himself.
>
> (1.1.52–60)

In this pretentious, Latinate style, Poet proceeds to tell the "moral" (1.1.90). Such "friends" (1.1.101) follow Timon to a high hill where he has "feigned Fortune to be throned" (1.1.64). When Fortune turns,

> all his dependents,
> Which labored after him to the mountain's top
> Even on their knees and hands, let him slip down,
> Not once accompanying his declining foot.
> (1.1.85–88)

Except for Timon's last misanthropic days, this is the play. Only the most sermon-loving of the audience would not have groaned at this stale fare (and there is no evidence that the play was ever performed before the Restoration). That the theme was of medieval, rather than vitally current emergence, is suggested in Painter's comment:

> 'Tis common.
> A thousand moral paintings I can show
> That shall demonstrate those quick blows of Fortune's
> More pregnantly than words.
>
> (1.1.89–92)

No one understood better than Shakespeare the need to animate old topics with drama. And so, indeed, he does combine with words many stage equivalents of "moral paintings." Each verbal bromide is preceded or followed by an enactment, an illustration. But for the first three acts, at least, action drags.

Normally, too, Shakespeare simply could not write of human beings without characterizing them, although in *Troilus and Cressida* he tried hard. In *Timon,* however, he not only tried hard but also succeeded. A glance at "The Actors' Names" is incriminating. After Timon's name comes Lucius, Lucullus, and Sempronius, bracketed together as "flattering lords." Then appears "Ventidius, one of Timon's false friends." These, it is true, will be more or less painted in action, and the flattering lords are at least as amusing as Jonson's "humor" characters. But throughout the listing are men without names, some of whom will be identified in the text but not in speech headings. Flavius, an important personage, is not listed, but he will later be referred to simply as Steward. Besides the nameless Poet and Painter, there are Jeweller and Merchant. Also in the text, but not elsewhere, is "Old Man." Senators, Lords, and Strangers are customarily listed as 1, 2, and 3. The namelessness and often featurelessness of so many personages is a characteristic of the moral play, in which type would not be (any more than "Old Man" here or in *King Lear*) threatened by individuality. We should also credit Shakespeare with knowledge of the popularity of the innumerable "characters" that were appearing in the early seventeenth century.

Besides the namelessness or the abstract quality of the characters, however, one must consider a comparable enemy of drama. This is the use of stereotypes for real figures. Timon would have been easily recognized as an archetypal misanthrope, if only from knowledge of a likely source for the play, Lucian's dialogue "Timon the Misanthrope."[7] The ubiquitous, but not amusing, Fool may be pardoned as certainly as Apemantus, "a churlish philosopher" whose vile harangues give vitality of language to much of the play. But Captain Alcibiades, who is vital to the ending, fits in almost every detail the mold of the "plain soldier," a graceless, rough-speaking figure who was becoming unavoidable in Jacobean drama. We shall see him given unprecedented dimensions and interest in Enobarbus and possibly in Coriolanus.

The insistent theme of the moral painting is not altogether an incubus. It is almost always figured forth in scenes. Additionally, the theme of fall from Fortune is varied by subsidiary, relevant themes. The trial of friendship is one of the most important (and current) motifs and leads to the penultimate theme of ingratitude and the ultimate bestial misanthropy of the final acts. Also—important and the first to appear—is the similarly current and vital theme of nobility.

The structure of the play, although it lacks the magnificent contrapuntal double plot of *Lear*, cannot be altogether dismissed as stiff. We have already briefly noticed its use of exempla and tableaux. Scenes are almost invariably structured by a series of comparable episodes. A scene illustrating the falling off of false friends consists, in sequence, of defections of the three flattering lords. The final scenes show that Timon must be played by a strong actor. In his cave he confronts a long series of visitors, most of whom he curses at length. These visitors seem to come by casually, yet uninterruptedly. It is significant that the crucial fifth act begins with the two sycophants, Poet and Painter, who had appeared at the beginning of act 1. All of this is artistry, not incomplete workmanship.

Especially deliberate in its design is the way the total play is organized, particularly if we employ modern, and generally accepted, divisions into acts and scenes. Besides the statement of "moral," all the major characters except for the steward Flavius are introduced in the first scene. More impressively, the acts are so ordered as to trace the steps in Timon's descent and also to focus, though not exclusively, upon one of the play's subsidiary themes. We can scarcely do better than to follow Shakespeare's method and order the subsequent sections of this chapter on the basis of his organization. But because his depiction of a theme does not usually begin or end neatly within its act, we must occasionally be true to his structure even in its lapses. Nobility, for example, though highlighting the first act, has later developments; and friendship, the motif of acts 2 and 3, is given intimations in act 1. This is proper because nobility and friendship are depicted as almost intertwining virtues.

Nobility

Noble vies with *beast* as the most frequently used word in the play. It names a quality that will be much talked about and exhibited. Appropriately act 1, with Timon at his zenith, is almost a spectacle of the loftiness, generosity, and largeness of spirit of this lord as he entertains in his house. There are, with a lavish banquet, significantly "loud music" (1.2) and a rising series of diversions and guests, extending from Poet and Painter to Alcibiades with some twenty horses and an assemblage of many ladies who dance.

Most noticeable, however, are Timon's suitors and his prompt attention to their requests. Poet and Painter are told to keep attendance, doubtless to be patronized. A messenger informs Timon of his friend Ventidius's imprisonment for a debt of five talents (by Shakespeare's calculation at this point a huge sum). The theme of friendship, as well as nobility, is illustrated by Timon's response. Not only will he help his friend up but the money will add enough to support him once he has risen. When Ventidius soon offers to repay Timon double because his father has bequeathed him riches, Timon declines the money; to accept would be to cheapen the relationship with ceremony, of which, "where there is true friendship" (1.2.18), none is needed. Apparently recognizing the close relationship of nobility and friendship, Ventidius exclaims, "A noble spirit!" (1.2.14). The hazardous dependence of nobility upon friendship is the only dark aspect of this act, and even that is displayed optimistically. "1. Lord" wishes that he and his fellow beneficiaries might adequately recompense by having Timon "once use our hearts" (1.2.80). The play is almost too compact of irony, and this is incisively present and disturbing in Timon's reassuring the lord that he will someday be able to use his fellows: "How had you been my friends else?" (1.2.85). The moral exchange is typically amplified verbally by Timon's lengthy disquisition linking noble giving to his friends' eagerness to help: "O what a precious comfort 'tis to have so many like brothers commanding one brother's fortunes!" (1.2.97–98). Another, more subtle irony comes when "2. Lord" observes of Timon that "No need but he repays / Sevenfold above itself" (1.1.274–75), and "1. Lord" comments in the key line of the scene: "The noblest mind he carries / That ever governed man" (1.1.277–78). The glow of the compliment is dimmed by the other lord's "Long may he live / In fortunes!" (1.1.278–79) as they proceed in subsequent acts to be inadequate to the almost total rejection by his friends. Apemantus, a Cynic, talks incessantly about the hollowness of the bounty and the feast. But he alone does so, and we need not accept as choric the cacophonous diatribes of this bitter character. Or is it possible that either Timon's nobility is flawed or to build a life on nobility is hazardous?

The answer depends to a large extent upon Renaissance definitions of this universally interesting virtue. Since not only *Timon* but also *Antony and Cleopatra* and *Coriolanus* are very concerned with achieving nobility, we should be at least aware of the subject as it was discussed in numbers of now rare books. And, as has been mentioned, the major source for the last two plays, and possibly for *Timon* (and Alcibiades), was North's translation of Plutarch's *Lives of the Noble Grecians and Romans*, a work dealing, as noted for *Julius Caesar*, with the nobility of the characters.

Probably the major aspect of these books was that they dealt with the *testing* of a person's nobility. One of the most popular of such works has the challenge implied in the title. This is Giovanni Battista Nenna's treatise, in dialogue form: *Nennio, or a Treatise of Nobility: Wherein is discussed what true nobilitie is*, translated in 1594 by William Jones (London, 1594). A comparable work in dramatic form was Henry Medwall's *Fulgens & Lucrece* (ca. 1497), a play based upon *De Vera Nobilitate*, a Latin *controversia* by Bonaccorso. Because so many of the works were in the form of a dialogue, a dispute, or a drama and were usually concerned with providing the answer to the question "What is true nobility?" we could predict the testing purpose of Shakespeare's plays dealing with the subject. Suggestive evidence is found in *Measure for Measure* when Angelo, hastily appointed Lord Deputy, makes the request whose full answer will be central to the play:

> Now, good my lord,
> Let there be some more test made of my mettle
> Before so noble and so great a figure
> Be stamp'd upon it.
>
> (1.1.47–50)

For Timon, the most telling evidence in his favor is that a primary connotation of *noble* was "respect for the common good," as Surrey expresses it in Shakespeare's *Henry VIII*. Moreover, this is a quality stressed by all didactic treatises. George Meriton—to take only one of many almost identical examples—in his *A Sermon of Nobilitie* (London, 1607) equates "a noble spirit" with a nature that is "directed not so much to private as to publicke good" (sig. E I'').

Whether or not Timon strictly meets this part of the test is debatable. His public service in the play is confined to giving of money. And he often seems to do so either excessively and ostentatiously or out of a need to be loved. In a difficult speech his steward laments his real poverty: "Nor will he know his purse, or yield me this, / To show him what a beggar his heart is, / Being of no power to make his wishes good" (1.2.188–90). Timon's heart may at bottom be a beggar, a beggar for approval. And it is one of the paradoxes of the play that he displays infinitely more an open purse than an open heart.

The second connotation of *nobility* is one we have already discussed briefly in *Julius Caesar*. Fundamentally it is a greatness of heart and courage. But there derives from this a noble recklessness or a noble trust in baser "metal" that makes one vulnerable. It is given "moral" expression by an ungrateful senator who is reported as saying, "a noble nature / May catch a wrench" (i.e., may meet reverses, 2.2.204–5). Shakespeare employs many examples of abused nobility. An earlier, important one is "the noble Moor" (*Oth.* 2.3.132). Iago hypocritically tells Othello: "I would not have your free and noble nature, / Out of self-bounty, be abused" (3.3.199–200). Resemblance to Timon in this accurate message is reinforced by the terms "self-bounty" and "free," both implying liberality. Nobility as generous credulity is found also outside Shakespeare. In *Euphues*,[8] John Lyly wrote, "the noble minde suspecteth no guile without cause, neither

condemneth any wight without proofe." And Ben Jonson in his dedication to *Volpone* similarly warned, "but let wise and noble persons
take heed how they be too credulous."[9] Fullest admiration for Timon's nobility may therefore require this meaning, which seems to
have had the loftiest application in Shakespeare before the last two
tragedies. It places Timon in the company of men like Brutus,
Othello, Antony, and Coriolanus. And by making his nobility one of
largeness of spirit, it makes his fall attributable to a flaw that is generous rather than meager-hearted.

Friendship

Acts 2 and 3 are mainly devoted to the testing of the virtue of
friendship. We are only too well prepared for it by the flatterers of
act 1 and by our awareness that nobility may have a "wrench" that
will futilely require help in adversity. And a common skepticism exists—not exempting ourselves—about disinterested motives for
friendship. The play certainly takes advantage of this skepticism and
thereby makes of Timon's final behavior something so deeply rooted
that it has been recognized in proverbs. One of these is used by
Flavius in his bitter mockery of how the "friends" speak:

> Great Timon; noble, worthy royal Timon!
> Ah, even the means are gone that buy this praise,
> The breath is gone whereof this praise is made.
> Feast-won, fast-lost.
>   (2.2.165–68)

Timon's fall is not subtly gradual. It is, rather, abruptly announced at the very beginning of act 2, when a senator describes Timon's huge debts to him and dispatches a servant to demand
payment. At Timon's house, the servant meets other servants similarly employed. When Flavius announces this reversal and its reason
to his master, Timon's response is typical of the rest of the play in
stating a theme that will presently be illustrated by a series of tableaux. He accounts these "wants" (2.2.178) as blessings; "for by
these / Shall I try friends" (2.2.179–80).

Like nobility, friendship had been copiously discussed in moral
philosophy; an entire book of *The Faerie Queene,* that superbly moral
allegory, had been devoted to it. Like nobility, too, a favorite topic

of the virtue was its trial. Only one typical work, savagely cynical about trusting friends, need be cited, for its title tells what may be found in many of the treatises. Written by one M. B. and published in 1596, the book is called *The Triall of True Friendship; or perfit mirror, whereby to discern a trustie friend from a flattering Parasite. Otherwise, a knacke to know a knave from an honest man: By a perfit mirrour of both: Soothly to say: Trie ere you trust; Believe no man rashly.* This scarcely subtle work is a sustained diatribe, taking up item by item ways in which false friends may disguise themselves and repeating ad nauseam the tests to be applied. These may all be essentially gathered under the rubric: "Do not trust." Such works obviously alerted Shakespeare's audience to the substance of acts 2 and 3. As the servant to Sempronius puts the results of Timon's trial of his friends, "My lord, / They have all been touched and found base metal, / For they have all denied him" (3.3.5–7). The imagery of assaying metal and finding it base links the themes of friendship and nobility.

Timon's passion in these acts is rendered noble also by the universal sympathy of the servants, both his and those of the ungrateful creditors. Flaminius after a rejection flings a proffered bribe at Lucullus, and comments, "O you gods, / I feel my master's passion" (3.1.52–53). Hortensius, on a collecting mission, says, "It is against my heart" (3.4.21). Besides the servants, three unnamed "Strangers" lament for Timon. That they are unnamed and unidentified certifies their disinterested authority. Observing the ingratitude "in every flatterer's spirit" (3.2.64), "1. Stranger" prepares for the later theme of worldwide misanthropy when he calls it "the world's soul" (3.2.63). The last acts are prepared for further when he adds, "O see the monstrousness of man / When he looks but in an ungrateful shape" (3.2.71–72). Except for a hysterical mock banquet, where he serves warm water and stones, Timon emerges creditably from these acts of false friendship. So weasel-like are the creditors that their defaulting can only make the fallen lord justified in fleeing Athens. Further is a servant's final comment: "This was my lord's best hope; now all are fled / Save only the gods" (3.3.35–36). And even the gods seem to have fled. Timon's change to Misanthropos is therefore not so abrupt as the change after act 1. Furthermore, he acts like a beast in flinging stones at the fleeing banquet guests. And he gives intimations of the crucial moral choice when he cries at them: "Burn house! Sink Athens! Henceforth hated be / Of Timon man and all humanity!" (3.6.101–2).

Misanthropos

Nevertheless, the final two acts are unprecedentedly violent ones, and their beginning marks an abrupt change not only in Timon's character but also in his speech. Speech and character are effectively joined in the change. Outside the walls of Athens, Timon introduces act 4 by a long harangue against all civilized and humane qualities of life. It would have been more characteristic of the carefully labeled structure of the play if Timon had first spoken a labeling line that he uses in the third scene: "I am Misanthropos and hate mankind" (4.3.54). But the longer speech, which usurps the entire first scene, is found enough to serve as a moral introduction. It is also fully explicit. And its prayerlike form is eminently suitable—as are similar invocations in *King Lear*—for an additional purpose: raising the tragic hero to more than an embittered individual, to an almost supernatural agent of wrath. The forty-one line speech is too long to be fully quoted here. Moreover, like Lear's even vaster prayerful curses, it needs to be heard. The language has the unmistakable power of Shakespeare's major plays. We know that, after the didactic stylized exposition of the first three acts, we are again at the mercy of the master and that the ending will be a much less easy one emotionally for us. A few lines from the speech will convey not only the majestic passion of the last two acts but also the Lear-like dependence of these acts upon an imperative mood and exclamation points.

These lines suggest the total intention of destroying all human institutions, proprieties, and feeling. After ordering a complete reversal of loyalties ("Matrons, turn incontinent! / Obedience fail in children! . . . / To general filths / Convert o' th' instant, green virginity!," 4.1.3–7), Timon waxes magnificent in eloquence and scope:

> Piety and fear,
> Religion to the gods, peace, justice, truth,
> Domestic awe, night-rest and neighborhood,
> Instruction, manners, mysteries and trades,
> Degrees, observances, customs and laws,
> Decline to your confounding contraries,
> And yet confusion live!
>   . . .
> Timon will to the woods, where he shall find
> Th' unkindest beast more kinder than mankind.
> The gods confound—hear me, you good gods all—

> Th' Athenians both within and out that wall;
> And grant, as Timon grows, his hate may grow
> To the whole race of mankind, high and low!
>
> (4.1.15–40)

There is a paradoxical piety in this curse; and it ends with a word that will give more than a note of destructive anger to the rest of the play: "Amen" (4.1.41). Except for the more titanic threats of *King Lear,* no play will force upon us a greater challenge to what sustains us: our humanity.

Shakespeare knew, moreover, that two acts of continuous misanthropy would not anxiously hold an audience made up—after all—of men versed from childhood in a fuller vision and moral heritage. Skillfully, therefore, he takes us immediately in the second scene back to Timon's house where, among the servants, we learn that humanity still exists. This reassuring episode may merely enhance the horror that we have witnessed. But it may—given Shakespeare's dramatic sense—be comparable to the Porter scene in *Macbeth,* giving us an author-controlled moment of release from horror.

It shows us that Timon's universal scourge of humankind is excessive. The servants are movingly loyal to their late master, and fellows still to one another. One servant mourns (in language far above the clownish style we are used to in servants) the friendless ruin of their master:

> Such a house broke?
> So noble a master fall'n; all gone, and not
> One friend to take his fortune by the arm
> And go along with him?
>
> (4.2.5–8)

And another reveals their tears: "Yet do our hearts wear Timon's livery; / That see I by our faces. We are fellows still, / Serving alike in sorrow" (4.2.17–19). Timon's influence in bringing men together in loyalty and love is further emphasized by the steward:

> Wherever we meet, for Timon's sake
> Let's yet be fellows; let's shake our heads and say,
> As 'twere a knell unto our master's fortunes,
> "We have seen better days."
>
> (4.2.24–27)

This sentiment will be soon undercut by Timon's behavior, naked and ugly, in his cave. He will never see what his servants see: "There's nothing level in our cursed natures / But direct villainy. Therefore be abhorred / All feasts, societies, and throngs of men" (4.3.19–21). His one moment of recognition, among those who visit him after he has found gold in the woods, will be from the behavior of his steward, who has come not to receive but to give gold. Timon can see by his tears that he does not belong to "flinty mankind" (4.3.480). And he is moved reluctantly to "proclaim / One honest man" (4.3.493). ·

With these dramatically useful exceptions to his misanthropy, the remainder of the play is nevertheless far from perfect. Even though the rest of the play is broken by interludes like these, not even Shakespeare can sustain for two acts the series of visitors whom Timon curses. There is, for example, far too long an exchange of "beast" (4.3.323) and "dog" (4.3.200) between him and Apemantus.

And, regrettably, the denouement of the play is not so much ethical as sociomilitary. Captain Alcibiades, who has been exiled for supporting a friend in trouble with the law, vows vengeance upon "the usuring Senate" (3.5.110). Timon gives him gold, but only to bring Athens to total ruin. In the final scene, ruin becomes almost a reality as Alcibiades advances upon Athens.

To the sound of trumpets, the Captain announces: "Sound to this coward and lascivious town / Our terrible approach" (5.4.1–2). And to the senators who appear upon the wall, his threat carries the indictment of one of Timon's curses, with a comparable language:

> Now the time is flush,
> When crouching marrow in the bearer strong
> Cries, of itself, "No more!" Now breathless wrong
> Shall sit and pant in your great chairs of ease
> And pursy insolence shall break his wind
> With fear and horrid flight.
>
>   (5.4.8–13)

Unlike Timon, Alcibiades is reasonable, and responds to the senators' plea to spare the innocent. "All have not offended" (5.4.36). Yet the scourging of the city is meant to be both realistic and symbolic. Alcibiades is less a character than a symbol of war (like Fortinbras), the kind of force the age believed always attendant upon a decadent city. It is significant that he uses the adjective "pursy" (or bloated and luxurious, 5.4.12) to describe the corrupt Athens, for Hamlet had used the same word to describe Denmark: "in the fatness of these pursy times" (*Ham* 3.4.154).

A purging of the state, with subsequent reordering, is a common ending in an Elizabethan play. Yet Shakespeare must have known that this purgation cannot embrace the major question: What about Timon? Timon has been liked by Alcibiades, and their fortunes and sufferings have been allied. Shakespeare could have vindicated his hero solely, but not totally, by Alcibiades's action and approval. But Timon remains unchanged, even now in his unexplained death and burial by the sea. One of his two epitaphs is as full of bitterness as ever: "Here lie I, Timon, who alive all living men did hate. / Pass by and curse thy fill; but pass, and stay not here thy gait" (5.4.72–73). The best that Shakespeare could do, or chose to do, in the way of justifying and enlarging Timon is to be found in the captain's final, extremely muted speech—the last of the play—commenting on the epitaph:

> These well express in thee thy latter spirits.
> Though thou abhorred'st in us our human griefs,
> Scorned'st our brains' flow and those droplets which
> From niggard nature fall, yet rich conceit
> Taught thee to make vast Neptune weep for aye
> On thy low grave, on faults forgiven. Dead
> Is noble Timon, of whose memory
> Hereafter more.
>
> (5.4.74–81)

Lear may utter his bestial "Howl, howl, howl" and revile "you men of stone" (5.3.257), yet for no heart do we feel more than for Lear's in his final ordeal. In his trial of passion, his heart grows as his fortunes decline. In drawing Timon, Shakespeare for the first time chose to paint a hero who turned to stone himself—a man who abhorred "in us our human griefs." It was also, with the much deepened exception of Coriolanus, the last time.

Chapter Ten
Antony and Cleopatra
This Dotage of Our General's

With no intended offense to Cleopatra, we must tell this love story, involving two extraordinary principals, first from the viewpoint of Antony. Cleopatra's turn—in a play of many turnings—must come later. But it is traditional, and in accordance with Shakespeare's deliberate structuring, to view the play as John Dryden titled it in his version: *All for Love: or, The World Well Lost;* and it is Antony who loses the world. In the underlying conflict between Rome and Egypt, all the Romans (who are, except for Cleopatra, the most formidable personages) lament the fall of Antony; they merely marvel at, to put it in its best light, the cunning of Cleopatra. The tragedy must, at least first of all, be seen as the disgrace and defeat of a Herculean hero.

And at the start, this hero is not, as some critics have rejoiced that he is, altogether a figure of magnificence. G. Wilson Knight, in a classical and well-titled essay, "The Transcendental Humanism of Antony and Cleopatra," deduces from the "thick-scattered 'world' references . . . [an] imperial magnificence and human nature is given no limited framework, as in *Lear*."[1] Similarly, a more disciplined scholar, Madeleine Doran, also in a perceptive and well-titled essay, "High Events as These: The Language of Hyperbole in *Antony and Cleopatra*," makes much of the first scene—particularly Antony's speech beginning "Let Rome in Tiber melt, and the wide arch / Of the ranged empire fall! Here is my space" (1.1.33–34). According to Miss Doran, this "speech immediately sets the tone of the play—the greatness of the issue, the sweep of the scene, the splendor of the imagery."[2] Mr. Knight would free Antony from "all natural limits." Similarly, Miss Doran, in calling attention to "the sweep of the scene," overlooks the ironic "Here is my space." (The "space" of Antony will turn out finally to be Cleopatra's monument.) Actually, the effect of the opening scene is to undercut the earlier magnificence of Antony, even while it comments at beginning and end on his present dotage. This first scene of the play is, much as *Timon of Athens,* in the form of a confining tableau. A typically Egyptian procession is announced: "Flourish. Enter Antony, Cleopatra, her Ladies, the Train, with Eunuchs fanning her." Apart from the Roman emperor Antony, these are the personages, with their "luxuriousness" (3.13.120) and sexual breadth and ambiguity, in whose company the ensnared Antony lives in Alexandria. Significantly, the first speaker in the play is Philo, one of Antony's two officers watching the scene. His long speech recalls the theme-setting formal description by Poet in *Timon*:

> Nay, but this dotage of our general's
> O'erflows the measure: those his godly eyes
> That o'er the files and musters of the war
> Have glowed like plated Mars, now bend, now turn
> The office and devotion of their view
> Upon a tawny front. His captain's heart,
> Which in the scuffles of great fights hath burst
> The buckles on his breast, reneges all temper
> And is become the bellows and the fan
> To cool a gypsy's lust.
>
> (1.1.1–10)

And as the group passes by, he adds: "Take but good note, and you shall see in him / The triple pillar of the world transformed / Into a strumpet's fool. Behold and see" (1.1.11–13). What we, the offstage audience, see, is a pair of middle-aged lovers protesting their passion and a playful quarrel. In their exchange, Antony expresses his total enslavement by derogating his empire: the amplitude of the world that is their "space." When the lovers and their train have passed, Demetrius, the other officer, joins Philo in his sorrows that Antony confirms "the common liar, who / Thus speaks of him at Rome" (1.1.60–61). Such, in brief, is the entire opening scene. Its structure is commentary with illustration. And its purpose is clearly not to glorify the doting Antony or the "gypsy" (4.12.28) or the "strumpet" (1.1.13). It is a "moral" and, though beautifully enacted, sad spectacle. The play is not usually praised for its random and scattered structure. Hence, it is the more remarkable that Shakespeare should open it so formally and didactically.

The idle, wanton behavior of Cleopatra's attendants in the second scene is not, moreover, calculated to glorify either Antony or Cleopatra. But later in the scene a messenger reports the urgent military need of Antony in Rome, and here begins the theme that will provide the major dramatic tension through most of act 2 and, in gradually weakened form, through the battles with Octavius Caesar. The theme supplies further moral gravity to the message of scene 1. It is simply whether or not Antony can free himself from sensual and idle bondage and once more be worthy to rule "the wide arch / Of the ranged empire" (1.1.33–34).

The effect of the messenger's challenging news is reflected in Cleopatra's all-too-knowing observation: "He was disposed to mirth; but on the sudden / A Roman thought hath struck him" (1.2.78–79). Rome, as is well recognized, stands in the play for military might, politic government, and discipline.

Antony's ordeal (it is at first only partially suffering) begins in earnest with this Roman thought. It is a thought of his nobility jeopardized: "These strong Egyptian fetters I must break / Or lose myself in dotage" (1.2.112–13). And again: "I must from this enchanting queen break off: / Ten thousand harms, more than the ills I know, / My idleness doth hatch" (1.2.124–26). And still again: "I must with haste from hence" (1.2.129).

The magnitude of the theme of struggle is almost entirely of Shakespeare's design. In general, the dramatist wisely and closely followed his source, Plutarch's *Lives*. Therein Antony had been given to debauchery since his youth. Consequently he is an easier prey to Cleopatra. Shakespeare has added not so much morality as dramatic tension to his opening acts by stressing what he was elsewhere so adept at stressing—inner struggle. Antony, however, must not be credited with special aptitude for what is fundamental in Brutus and Hamlet. Shakespeare not only provides drama early in the play. The struggle will have a lingering and poignant afterlife once Antony has decided, in his moral choice, to give up the struggle; it will give him his major source of suffering after his total surrender to Cleopatra.

All the Roman soldiers follow Philo and Demetrius in trying to rescue Antony. The most interesting of these, Enobarbus, is not so morally or militarily simple as the first two. Of all the characters, he has the most perceptive and even appreciative view of the "enchanting queen" (1.2.124). He seems to be trying to persuade his master not to leave her or Egypt, though actually he is taunting Antony by praising her "celerity in dying" (1.2.141). He knows, cynical though he may be, the ways of women as the totally infatuated Antony cannot. It is to him that Shakespeare assigns the most famous passage in the play, that describing the first meeting of Antony and Cleopatra at the Cydnus when she is on her barge (2.2.191–219).

The speech is made to captains of Caesar and Lepidus when Enobarbus and Antony have finally gone to Rome. But it does not stand alone in his witty but admiring accounts about the Queen to these hardened veterans. When a peace between Caesar and Antony has been tenuously fabricated by Antony's marriage to Caesar's sister Octavia, the officers comment upon the likelihood of Antony's permanently leaving Cleopatra. Caesar's Maecenas is naive: "Now Antony must leave her utterly" (2.2.234). Enobarbus knows even better than Antony the truth:

> Never; he will not:
> Age cannot wither her, nor custom stale
> Her infinite variety: other women cloy
> The appetites they feed, but she makes hungry
> Where most she satisfies.
>
> (2.2.235–39)

It is in the next scene that Enobarbus is proved correct. From the Soothsayer, Antony gains confirmation that, when apart from Caesar, his "spirit" is "noble, courageous, high, unmatchable" (2.3.19–20). But near him, he loses. Antony recognizes the truth of all the evidence the Soothsayer presents; but, alone, he gives the real reason that he will leave Rome: "I will to Egypt: / And though I make this marriage for my peace, / I'th East my pleasure lies" (2.3.38–40).

This is his great moral crisis, and it also, by more than abject surrender, concludes the struggle. Just as Antony will kill himself, will make the wrong decisions about Pompey and about the battles at Actium, so he is always responsible, sometimes heroically, for his own fate. His yielding to Cleopatra is, to be sure, "sickening" (3.10.16) to Enobarbus when she leads Antony in shameful retreat. And Cleopatra is often referred to as an enchantress, as a "fairy" (4.8.12), "witch" (4.12.47), or "charm" (4.12.16), suggesting that, like the Soothsayer, she is capable of the supernatural. But as we view her human side more closely, and as we see the less noble infidelity of Antony, we will recognize that Shakespeare, in giving him a moral struggle, was not unfaithful to his habit of making his protagonist heroically responsible enough to be great.

Defection and Loyalty

In the contrast between East and West, it has been convenient and attractive for readers to look upon Cleopatra's world as one of fickleness and change. She, the embodiment of her country's temperament, is "cunning past man's thought" (1.2.142). She has had a succession of lovers—specializing in world leaders. Antony, in rage at her allowing Caesar's emissary Thidias to kiss her hand, storms at her erotic versatility. Accusing her of having "been a boggler [ie., shifty one] ever" (3.13.110), he berates what Enobarbus appreciatively calls "her infinite variety":

> I found you as a morsel cold upon
> Dead Caesar's trencher: nay, you were a fragment
> Of Gneius Pompey's, besides what hotter hours,
> Unregist'red in vulgar fame, you have
> Luxuriously picked out. For I am sure,
> Though you can guess what temperance should be,
> You know not what it is.
>
> (3.13.116–22)

At this late point in the play, her willingness to remain dangerously true to Antony is shaky, and we shall subsequently take this into account. Moreover, nearly until act 5 she has little moral sense, or "temperance." But it would be more in keeping with her genuine ardor to call her amoral rather than immoral. And as for her court generally, though they have more sense of wanton play than of honor, her women with her in her final episodes are movingly loyal.

It is not our intention to deprive readers of their righteous pleasure in the comedy, ribaldry, and morally free conduct of the Egyptians. Indeed, however indignant we may be at Egyptian perfidy in battle, much of our benefit from the play comes not from moral issues but from their opposite. As with Falstaff, we are for more than a two-hour traffic liberated from moral imperatives and can abandon ourselves to a world in which tyrannical loyalties are allowed to "melt" (4.12.22).

But we do not need to exonerate the Egyptians entirely for this reason. We need to look at the Romans, both those under Antony and those under Caesar and Pompey, in order to question the stereotyped East-West dichotomy. Granted their greater devotion to the world of duty and business, just how loyal are these Romans? Can they be, though not so "luxurious" (3.13.120) as the Egyptians, any less slippery?

That they can be, in good measure, is manifest in their degree of loyalty to Antony, which Shakespeare assesses and dramatizes in nearly half of the play. This is important for the role of suffering, for, as noticed, the tragedy is unusually free from the customary causes of this important emotion. It is in responding to defection that Antony "continues still a Jove" (4.6.29). His suffering helps to define his basic and varied nature. He can rage like Hercules; he can be his old theatrical self, dramatizing his plight so that his friends weep; or he can more fundamentally be his majestic self, noble in loss.

To return to Roman loyalty, it is with Antony that we must begin. In scene three, when Antony informs Cleopatra that he is returning to Rome, she is so cunning that it would be profanation to defend her from a charge of trickiness. She appalls even Charmian with her perverse strategy for holding onto a man. She will die at the news: "the sides of nature / Will not sustain it" (1.3.16–17). There is a superb playing of the abused mistress when she asks Antony: "What, says the married woman you may go?" (1.3.20). But one ardently poetic speech, superior to any action of the two lovers, redeems her and cheapens Antony. It is a thrilling manifesto of a former loyalty:

> Nay, pray you seek no color for your going,
> But bid farewell, and go: When you sued staying
> Then was the time for words: no going then,
> Eternity was in our lips and eyes,
> Bliss in our brows' bent.
>
> (1.3.32–36)

Antony is surely aware that he will defect, but he betrays a cunning—not poetic but falsely prosaic—in "my full heart / Remains in use with you" (1.3.43–44). Her subsequent tantrum with the messenger bearing news of Antony's marriage with Octavia may be pettily misplaced, but it is genuine. And once she has vented her fury, she rises to a sense of shame that makes her seem superior to the man who has rejected her: "These hands do lack nobility, that strike / A meaner than myself" (2.5.82–83). Antony will later call his mistress an undeservedly "Triple-turned whore" (4.12.13). But the expression of hurt pride could be applied equally well to Antony himself, for he has triple-turned from Fulvia, to Cleopatra, and now to Octavia.

The defection of Antony is proposed by Agrippa, another Roman.

Antony scarcely hesitates in casting off as an "Egyptian dish" (2.6.123) one who so loves him. In marrying not for love but for policy, he is being grossly untrue to one who has only herself to offer, and it seems cruel to regard her only as a carnal object. Only the hard-hearted soldiers of Pompey and Caesar can see the shameful opportunism in the marriage; even Cleopatra's "slippery" (1.2.181) women do not comment on it. Menas correctly, but without moral reproof, diagnoses the union: "I think the policy of that purpose made more in marriage than the love of the parties" (2.6.115–16). Enobarbus agrees: "He married but his occasion here" (2.6.127–28).

Antony's next defection is from his but recently married Octavia. This perhaps too quiet woman tries vainly to hold her husband and the marriage that means much to her. To her credit, she takes with generous sadness Antony's announcement, and even tries to clear Antony with Caesar. She is, of course, not an Egyptian, but she, with her "holy, cold, and still conversation" (2.6.119–20), is not much more admirable—perhaps less marvelous—in separation than her Egyptian predecessor.

It is not Antony only among the Romans who defects. Opportunism and disloyalty taint a majority of the high-ranking officers. The first incident is perhaps the defection that spells out the motif for the play, as well as the military fall of Antony. This is only a premonition of later leaving. On Pompey's galley, ironically during an orgy celebrating the peace and union with the famous pirate, Pompey's lieutenant Menas draws him aside and proposes a shameful stratagem: Cut the cable of the barge, cut the throats of the drunken world-sharers, and then "All there is thine" (2.7.72). Pompey rejects the stratagem, but not for honorable reasons: "Ah, this thou shouldst have done / And not spoke on't. In me 'tis villainy, / In thee't had been good service" (2.7.72–74). Pompey's political baseness is exceeded by that of his lieutenant. In an aside, Menas accurately foreshadows ensuing disloyalties:

> For this,
> I'll never follow thy palled fortunes more,
> Who seeks, and will not take when once 'tis offered,
> Shall never find it more.
> (2.7.80–83)

"Palled fortunes" will be a motive of virtually every major action in Antony's downfall as well. It is not so, however, in the conduct of his lieutenant general Ventidius: first, because Antony is not then losing; and second, because Ventidius in winning expresses not only a defection but also the corrupt opportunism of Antony's leaders. Having won a major victory for Antony in Syria, Silvius urges him to the obvious military move: "The fugitive Parthians follow" (3.1.7). Ventidius refuses:

> A lower place, note well,
> May make too great an act . . . .
> Who does i' th' wars more than his captain can
> Becomes his captain's captain.
>
> (3.1.12–22)

The scene (3.1) is brief, and its obvious purpose is to illustrate what Plutarch in his long narrative can do: make impressive the wide range of the empire that Antony is losing. But it also is strong with the underlying political cunning of the Romans. Ventidius is only in cold reasoning and "fortune" (3.1.2) superior to the numerous captains who will leave Antony. And his cold reason is evidenced by what he says of another lieutenant who, "For quick accumulation of renown, / Which he achieved by th' minute, lost his favor" (3.1.19–20).

The battle scenes are especially thick with desertions. The two losses are of course mainly because of Antony's resumed dotage to Cleopatra. But it is what follows the losses that shows the Romans in true color. Scarus, the stalwart soldier who would fight by land, is almost alone loyal. Shakespeare reverses Plutarch and makes him true, even though he has every reason to leave his general. The reporting rather than the enactment of the sea fight makes it possible for the soldiers to pass judgment. Scarus, referring to Antony as "the noble ruin of her magic" (3.10.19), comments: "I never saw an action of such shame; / Experience, manhood, honor, ne'er before / Did so violate itself" (3.10.22–24).

Scarus's loyalty will find a near, but more complex, parallel in Enobarbus. This soldier, Antony's good friend, whose "eyes did sicken at the sight" (3.10.16), is the most important commentator on the actions of his fellows. Because he seems to be a battle-wise, even skeptical soldier, his observations are shrewd. Canidius, Antony's lieutenant general, shiftily justifies his own disastrous desertion: "O, he has given example for our flight / Most grossly by his own" (3.10.29–30). Enobarbus's aside is keen: "Ay, are you thereabouts? / Why then, good night indeed" (3.10.29–30). Though keen in insight, however, he personally resolves to follow Antony's "wounded chance . . . . though my reason / Sits in the wind against me" (3.10.36–37). His struggle between loyalty and reason will be subsequently expressed several times, culminating in his observation of Cleopatra's seeming to heed Thidias's approaches. This struggle is one of central importance. It shows the supposed strongest advocate of reason trying to find rational grounds for loyalty when his comrades have defaulted, not out of reason but out of expediency.

But on a higher dramatic scale, Enobarbus's struggle provides three of the most brilliantly drawn scenes in the course of Antony's downfall. It provides them, moreover, when the "lated" (3.11.3) emperor most needs favorable evidence to make him "Antony yet" (3.13.93). First, a soldier informs the Emperor of Enobarbus's desertion. Then Eros lets him know that the fugitive has left "his chests and treasure" (4.5.10). A lesser man would have bitterly confiscated the possessions and turned from his trusted friend. It is testimony to Antony's largeness, especially during his later ordeal, that he orders the treasure sent to Enobarbus in Caesar's camp with the "wish he never find more cause / To change a master" (4.5.15–16). In the next scene, the ordeal is movingly that of Enobarbus:

> O Antony,
> Thou mine of bounty, how wouldst thou have paid
> My better service, when my turpitude
> Thou dost so crown with gold! This blows my heart.
> If swift thought break it not, a swifter mean
> Shall outstrike thought; but thought will do't, I feel.
>
> (4.6.31–36)

In a final episode Enobarbus, in a ditch, resolves to die of a broken heart:

> Throw my heart
> Against the flint and hardness of my fault,
> Which, being dried with grief, will break to powder,
> And finish all foul thoughts.
>
> (4.9.15–18)

Thus does the most level-headed of Romans perish of grief, and thus is Antony uplifted, all the more so because he stands apart from the Roman opportunists.

Even Romans on the other side behave dishonorably. Caesar himself, a supposed model of integrity, has Lepidus jailed on trumped-up charges. He craftily gives Thidias free rein in any cunning or false way to ensnare Cleopatra. And Caesar's Proculeius, whom the dying Antony had advised Cleopatra among Caesar's men alone to trust, is the agent whereby she is captured in her monument.

That she seeks still her honor in her last days, even while Caesar is dishonorably seeking his, provides further contrast that cheapens Roman integrity. Additionally, Cleopatra, as Linda Fitz [Woodbridge][3] has suggested in a disconcertingly fresh (and feminist) essay, is not playing false games simply to keep Antony in dotage. The Queen's cunning stratagems may be her only way to hold to her a man she genuinely loves. She cannot, we may add, succeed against the militarily formidable, but not altogether honorable, Romans by trying to be the capable monarch that she is in Plutarch. There is a brave attempt at this role when she reviles Enobarbus for trying to keep her presence from the war:

> Sink Rome, and their tongues rot
> That speak against us! A charge we bear i'th'war,
> And as the president of my kingdom will
> Appear there for a man.
>
> (3.7.15–18)

Soon she will have to apologize for her "fearful sails" (3.11.55); but there is in her, at least toward the end of the play, an attempt not only to honor but also to match the nobility of her fallen Antony. The nobility blends in meaning with loyalty. It becomes, in fact, the measure of her true greatness—as of her fundamental seriousness— and it is to this virtue that we must finally turn. Almost alone it will, if the lovers meet the traditional challenge, justify the passion of the two monarchs as something more than an entertainment of game and betrayal.

The Nobleness of Life

We may still hold—if only because it makes the most of Cleopatra's infinite variety—the traditional view of tricky, debauched Egypt. More confidently, however, we may differentiate the two worlds, Rome and Egypt, on their relative nobility. Like all the Roman plays, this tragedy achieves final meaning and glory by highlighting the protagonists' meeting of the traditional challenge just mentioned and more fully defined in the chapter on *Timon of Athens*. Here, however, we have two protagonists, one of them an Egyptian. Shakespeare makes fullest dramatic capital not only by assessing Antony's final nobility; he also, typically, plays for the highest stakes by doing the seemingly impossible: showing us a noble Egyptian.

Noble in this tragedy has a complex of applications—greater than that which treatises on the subject had simplified into a public servant or into a large, often vulnerably so, figure so suitable for tragedy. Here it spreads out in many directions from the Latin root meaning "renown." It naturally denotes fame, honor, and magnificence. Its meaning is often defined by its opposite of base, ordinary, or cheap; and Shakespeare is seldom unaware of its monetary meaning in terms of a precious metal. Hence, as in *Timon,* bounteousness is one of its qualities. Its possessor will be generous and large in his actions. But perhaps greatness of heart and spirit, always implying courage, will underlie the term. The word itself is used more than any other at the conclusion of the tragedy, but there is seldom any question as to its quality when the word is not used but merely implied. Hence, one of the most telling descriptions is in Cleopatra's trance-like, and hence deep, portrayal of her dead lover to Dolabella:

> His legs bestrid the ocean: his reared arm
> Crested the world: his voice was propertied
> As all the tuned spheres, and that to friends;
> But when he meant to quail and shake the orb,
> He was as rattling thunder. For his bounty,
> There was no winter in't: an autumn 'twas
> That grew the more by reaping: his delights
> Were dolphin-like, they showed his back above
> The element they lived in: in his livery
> Walked crowns and crownets: realms and islands were
> As plates dropped from his pocket.
>
> (5.2.82–92)

No other character in Shakespeare is so generously drawn. And it is no accident that this amplitude of soul is figured forth in words that best exemplify Coleridge's name for the language in the play: "a happy valiancy of style" ("Feliciter Audax").[4]

At the play's beginning there is little of this style. In the first scene, however, there is an episode of thematic importance. Antony, embracing Cleopatra, renounces the ranged empire in her favor:

"Kingdoms are clay: our dungy earth alike / Feeds beast as man. The nobleness of life / Is to do thus" (1.1.35–37). Usually in Shakespeare the equation of beast and man would have been ominous. More so would be the carnal definition of the "nobleness of life." Carnality is certainly not an ideal in Hamlet's "how noble in reason" (*Ham* 2.2.300). Nor is it so in Nenna's remarks on nobility and reason: "true and perfect nobilitie of man, consisteth only in that part, which maked man different from beastes; and that is reason" (sig. V 3ʳ). If we are as puritanical as George Bernard Shaw, we would take the episode, as Philo and Demetrius do, as an intimation of the beastlike fall that will occur. But, despite Shaw, poetry in the play does not always elevate by orchestrating a basically cheap sentiment.[5] And this is indeed poetry, and the kind whose thrill is not meant to disguise prose. In a world populated by self-seeking political leaders, a world of opportunism rather than loyalty, we are ourselves ignoble if we do not thrill to the heartfelt dedication of this mutual pair.

It is near the end of act 3, after the first defeat in battle, that this nobleness of life will be tested, and tested by a valiant blending of feeling and poetry. For curiously it is not during the lovers' high fortunes but during their adversity that nobility will be the key word and the dominating issue. But this is not un-Shakespearean. In so different yet strangely akin a play as *King Lear,* the protagonist will not learn to be a king until he loses his crown. Cleopatra will not even learn the meaning of nobility until she sees it in Antony's death.

Antony first defines the later tragic meaning of nobility after his loss at Actium. His usage implies its opposite: tainted reputation and instability of courage: "I have offended reputation, / A most unnoble swerving" (3.11.49–50). Both integrity and reputation are basic ingredients in Enobarbus' recognition, in his own swearings of his baseness and Antony's nobility. And there is in this episode a deeply realized feeling of his master's bounty: "O Antony, / Nobler than my revolt is infamous" (4.9.18–19).

In Antony's decline, there begins both a heroically grand suffering and a swelling eloquence lamenting his threatened loss of nobility. The former is dominant first in his noble display of Herculean agony. Charmian advises the frightened Cleopatra, after his last defeat:

> To th' monument!
> There lock yourself, and send him word you are dead.
> The soul and body rive not more in parting
> Than greatness going off.
>
> (4.13.6–9)

The latter develops when his rage is transfigured into a new nobleness of life after he (falsely) learns that Cleopatra is dead.

Increasingly, he seeks his rightful identity by reflecting on what Matthew Proser[6] has called his "heroic image": "Apace, Eros, apace. / No more a soldier. Bruised pieces, go; / You have been nobly borne" (4.14.41–43).

Joined with this search now is the challenge of his present nobility made by what he considers Cleopatra's superior nobility in dying. (In his own nobility he never learns Enobarbus's observation, "I have seen her die twenty times upon far poorer moment," 1.2.138–39.) With his own absorption in Roman nobility, he credits the "gypsy" with a nobility that she will only later receive, while he remains dishonorably alive and "base":

> Since Cleopatra died
> I have lived in such dishonor that the gods
> Detest my baseness. I, that with my sword
> Quartered the world and o'er green Neptune's back
> With ships made cities, condemn myself to lack
> The courage of a woman—less noble mind
> Than she which by her death our Caesar tells
> "I am conqueror of myself."
>
> (4.14.55–62)

His quest for final nobility is aided by the devotion (so rare at this point) of Eros, a name meaning "love." Eros, requested to kill his master, tells him to "Turn from me then that noble countenance / Wherein the worship of the whole world lies" (4.14.85–86). But instead of killing his master, Eros kills himself. Antony now has two persons who lead him on the course once taken by Brutus and Cassius:

> Thrice-nobler than myself!
> Thou teachest me, O valiant Eros, what
> I should, and thou couldst not. My queen and Eros
> Have by their brave instruction got upon me
> A nobleness in record. But I will be
> A bridegroom in my death, and run into't
> As to a lover's bed.
>
> (4.14.95–101)

There is a mixture of nobility and eroticism in his resolution, and it is not inappropriate that his falling on his sword (shown by Maurice Charney to have become a symbol of impotence)[7] should be at first a bungled death. None of his attendants will help him to end his life, and one of them, Decretas, even takes his sword to Caesar to get his favor. The lovers, depite Eros, are still in "a vile world" (5.2.313). Guardsmen do, however, take him to the monument of the still much alive Cleopatra. There, as Antony is dying, he joins his queen in eulogizing himself in terms of nobility. Earlier, in his good fortunes, he had sternly warned a messenger, "Things that are past are done with me" (1.2.93). Later, however, he must look back upon greatness. He sends word to Caesar that he makes him mad by thinking of him as he is now and not as he used to be. And he tries to turn Cleopatra's eyes from his present shame "By looking back what I have left behind / 'Stroyed in dishonor" (3.11.53–54). So now, with a sense of theater that never left him after *Julius Caesar*, he tries to keep his noble image in her mind by looking back.

There is an operatic opulence, and even some melodrama, in his death scene. His repeated "I am dying, Egypt, dying" (4.14.19,41) is theatrical. Nor is the nobility of this scene enhanced by the bungled attempt at death. But, inflated by rhetoric though his final words may be, and the sense of nobility flawed by vanity, we and Cleopatra respond to his self-eulogy:

> The miserable change now at my end
> Lament nor sorrow at; but please your thoughts
> In feeding them with those my former fortunes,
> Wherein I lived the greatest prince o' th' world,
> The noblest: and do now not basely die,
> Not cowardly put off my helmet to
> My countryman. A Roman, by a Roman
> Valiantly vanquished.
>
> (4.15.51–58)

As he dies, she is equally "valiant" in style, in the well-known, sensuous, yet imperial, speech, that follows her "Noblest of men, woo't die?" (4.15.59). Her greatest tribute to her dead lover comes shortly:

> Why, how now, Charmian?
> My noble girls! Ah, women, women, look!
> Our lamp is spent, it's out! Good sirs, take heart:

We'll bury him; and then, what's brave, what's noble,
Let's do't after the high Roman fashion,
And make death proud to take us.

                                    (4.15.86–91)

The verse is exalted, but what is remarkable is its prose message—if
Cleopatra in passion can have a prose. The message is, in tribute to
"This case of that huge spirit" (4.15.92), that she will observe the
high Roman fashion and do what is noble. Her essential knowledge
of Roman nobility may be shaky. Nor is she really qualified ever to
learn it. But she does know that she must follow Antony in death.
The struggle to be so noble will be the remainder of her life. And it
is a struggle as worthy of tragic stature as her infinite variety was of
her wanton days. Shakespeare has given her the whole fifth act, and,
as Willard Farnham says, she makes the most of it.

She withstands temptations from Caesar, though in her own in-
scrutable way. She grasps one aspect of nobility when she realizes the
actual paltriness of Caesar. Her perception is promptly illustrated by
the words of Proculeius, who has come with blandishments (and soldiers) to seduce her. What Proculeius reports of Caesar's intention
seems like a paltry echo of Antony's nobility:

                    Cleopatra,
        Do not abuse my master's bounty by
        Th' undoing of yourself: let the world see
        His nobleness well acted, which your death
        Will never let come forth.

                                    (5.2.42–46)

Caesar's direct approaches she easily sees through, even though they
are more dangerous to her and her family: "He words me, girls, he
words me, that I should not / Be noble to myself!" (5.2.191–92). She
even tries—fortunately—to be "no more but e'en a woman"
(4.15.76). We must remember—and she does not finally let us forget—that even in a noble death she *is* a woman under the formidable
control of alien men. She will try briefly to "shackle accidents and
bolt up change" (5.2.6). She will say of the asp:

                    What poor an instrument
        May do a noble deed! He brings me liberty.
        My resolution's placed, and I have nothing
        Of woman in me.

                                    (5.2.236–39)

It is with fiercer resolution that Lady Macbeth had tried to be both more and less than woman. Neither succeeds, especially Cleopatra.

It is as a queenly woman that she will meet death. As she has her costume prepared for dying, she is celebrating a bridal: "Husband, I come" (5.2.286). And she sees Antony "rouse himself / To praise my noble act" (5.2.283–84). She must give up, to be worthy of using the name of husband, all the elements of "baser life" (5.2.289). But her death is replete with sexual imagery of the bridal chamber. Perhaps her mingled femininity and claim to Roman nobility is best expressed by Caesar when he sees her in death: "O noble weakness!" (5.2.342).

Maynard Mack's use of Meredith's sonnet[8] to describe the complexity and contradictions of the play is felicitous: "Those who would have the play otherwise," he writes, "who are hot for certainties in this our life, . . should turn to authors other than Shakespeare, and should have been born into some other world than this." But if we regrettably cannot follow the latter piece of advice, we can find an author—Shakespeare himself—who can at least allay some of our heat for certainties. Shakespeare usually entrusts his final message to the person of highest rank, in this case the judicious if not lovable Caesar:

> Take up her bed,
> And bear her women from the monument.
> She shall be buried by her Antony.
> No grave upon the earth shall clip in it
> A pair so famous. High events as these
> Strike those that make them; and their story is
> No less in pity than his glory which
> Brought them to be lamented.
>
> (5.2.354–61)

We have, after all, witnessed—if not the clear spectacle nauseating to Shaw—at least a story bringing together two civilizations and two sexes in the most famous of all "pairs." Through a tragedy of "high events," Shakespeare has created more than uncertainties: he has eternally united this pair in nobility. There is prescience in Cleopatra's "immortal longings" (5.2.280).

Chapter Eleven

Coriolanus

Last of the Roman Trilogy

Following within a year of *Antony and Cleopatra*, and presumably Shakespeare's last tragedy, *Coriolanus*, like that play and *Julius Caesar*, is based closely upon Plutarch and upon Rome. Shakespeare seemingly found in his richest source—to view the situation most skeptically—character, episode, and language that he could most easily use. If so, this was the highest tribute that any historian has ever received. A still greater tribute to Plutarch, and the more likely reason that Shakespeare so devotedly used the Greek historian, was that the dramatist became in his last tragic period compellingly interested in what Plutarch taught him about Rome and nobility.

It is, of course, not unusual for an author to write a series of works on a subject, often set in the same locale. Today we have "trios" or "quartets" or even longer series by novelists like John Galsworthy, Lawrence Durrell, C. P. Snow, Anthony Burgess, and Paul Scott. Shakespeare himself had written two tetralogies on English history. With the Roman trilogy, the motive was not to complete a story (though *Antony* carries on from *Julius Caesar*) but to explore more fully the glory that was Rome. And one subject that persists from the first to the third is the quality of nobility. This, as we have noted, is in large part due to Plutarch's inspiration. But it was also generally recognized in Shakespeare's England that the virtue most valued among the Romans was nobility. Rome was, according to Osorio da Fonsceca, "the noblest city that ever was."[1] "The high Roman fashion" (*AC* 4.15.90), to use Cleopatra's phrase, came from "what's brave, what's noble" (4.15.89). These qualities lent themselves to characters heroically suited to high tragedy. They lent themselves also to probing inquiries into true nobility. The age was, after all—or so Spenser among many demonstrates—as much interested in books depicting virtues as in those about actual personages. But it was also, like Shakespeare, interested in the body politic, an arena in which these virtues might be shown in nonallegorical action. Hence, as

Harry Levin has written, all three of the Roman plays "constitute a great debate on ethics, in which the statement of private interests is balanced against the counter-statement of public responsibilities."[2]

Patricians and Plebeians

Coriolanus is as much concerned with the nobility of noblemen as it is with the virtue. Shakespeare makes the best of both worlds. For the foremost nobles are made interesting by individual traits, even as they exemplify, with one great exception, how a nobleman should behave. The same cannot be said of the commoners. These are introduced at the beginning in a riot not unfamiliar to readers of *Julius Caesar*. They stink, have greasy caps that they throw in the air, are fickle, and complain of their poverty. With two exceptions, they are known simply as First Citizen and Second Citizen. These two exceptions are the tribunes of the people, Sicinius and Brutus, who owe their offices to the nobility's attempt to placate the people. They are mean, crafty old men who are calculated to be "foes to nobleness" (3.1.45) and a major cause of Coriolanus's tragedy (*Coriolanus* being the honorific name given to Caius Marcius after his heroism at Corioli, 1.9.64).

However appreciative Shakespeare may have been of Plutarch's interpretation, there were limits—set partially by his theme and partially by his Elizabethan persuasions—beyond which he could not go in loyalty to his source. If he could sharpen conflicts or make factions more intelligible to his audience, he seldom hesitated to do so. He was more the dramatist than a conscientious historian, as students of *Richard III* know only too well. In *Coriolanus*, his persistent interest is in assessing the relative worth to Rome of the nobility and the commonalty. He makes the contrast more dramatic—yet somehow not too obvious—by debasing the commonalty and by intensifying the patrician qualities of the nobles. But he succeeds also in giving a balanced picture by concentrating the class loyalties upon one or two characters.

The plebs are, to be sure, made more raucous and stupid than in Plutarch. In the historian's version there is no rioting. The poor people protest not an inequity of wealth but an inability to grow grain because of incessant wars. Instead of using staves, they quietly encamp themselves in protest on a "sacred mount."[3] Unlike Shakespeare's citizens, they have fought for their country. Shakespeare does not make them evil; he has them calmly discuss the vices and virtues of the nobles and particularly of Coriolanus. What they lack in stereotyping, however, is more than recompensed by the base cunning of their leaders and their stupid herdlike behavior under the leaders' prodding.

The patricians, on the other hand, are reported to be unkind and ungenerous to the people. But they are level-headed, particularly Menenius,"a humorous patrician" (2.1.43) whom they like and to whose tedious tale of the Belly and the Members they patiently listen. He quiets their complaints until the brusque entrance of Caius Marcius, whose curses on the people arouse them again. Marcius has been changed by Shakespeare as much as the plebs. In Plutarch, he is not so much the aristocratic ruffian or the fierce soldier. His roughness is attributed to his being an orphan and growing up ill-educated. In spite of these handicaps, he has acquired an eloquence, contrasting sharply with the harshness of tongue that in Shakespeare is attributed to his conventional soldierly disabilities.

As in two other of the last tragedies, there is a strong female lead. This is Volumnia, Coriolanus's mother. She has had no other child, and she has devoted her life to her son, even as she has demanded all from him. It is to her formidable influence that he owes his pride in war and caste, though she denies credit for this pride. Their relationship will prove to be an ardent one, and probably the one immediate cause of his tragedy. She is the kind of mother-in-law that wives fear most. It is more than a Freudian slip when, in rejoicing that her son is at war with the Volscians, she tells his wife, Virgilia:

If my son were my husband, I should freelier rejoice in that absence where-in he won honor than in the embracements of his bed where he would show most love. When yet he was but tender-bodied and the only son of my womb, when youth with comeliness plucked all gaze his way, when for a day of kings' entreaties a mother should not sell him an hour from her beholding, I, considering how honor would become such a person, that it was no better than picture-like to hang by th' wall, if renown made it not stir, was pleased to let him seek danger where he was like to find fame. To a cruel war I sent him, from whence he returned, his brows bound with oak. (1.3.2–14)

And her indomitable passion for his nobility is strong in "I had rather had eleven [sons] die nobly for their country than one voluptuously surfeit out of action" (1.3.21–23). Like her son, she detests the rabble, but her instructions fail to teach him her tact. He becomes of a nature "too noble for the world" (3.1.255).

Too Noble for the World

Although he is too fierce and fights too much like a "lonely dragon" (4.1.30) to make an ideal general, Marcius succeeds by wrathful force in subduing Rome's Volscian enemies. In particular, he drives off his greatest foreign enemy, Tullus Aufidius, and in an Elizabethan, but not Roman action, he alone enters the gates of Corioli—an action that audiences would have misgivingly associated with Sir Richard Grenville. His return to Rome is one of hysterical tribute to a war hero. Had he been permitted to function only in war, where he can safely "sweat with wrath" (1.4.27), there would have been no tragedy. But his mother and noble friends have civil ambitions for him: he must, against his true intuition, stand for consul, though he "had rather be [the people's] servant in my way / Than sway with them in theirs" (2.1.192–93).

His love for his country may be genuine. And certainly in serving his country in war he is meeting a primary prescription for true nobility—one we have glanced at in *Timon*. This is a prescription that is usually contrasted in treatises with merely noble birth. Spenser's sonnet prefacing Jones's *Nennio* emphasizes that it is a book for

> Whoso wil seeke by right deserts t' attaine
> Unto the type of true Nobility
> And not painted shews & titles vaine,
> Derived farre from famous Ancestrie.

And Henry Peacham defines nobility as the distinction conferred upon men who, through "some glorious Action performed," have "been usefull and beneficiall to the common-wealthes and places where they live."[4] Coriolanus knows and probably feels this creed. It is why he will not accept material honors for his Corioli heroism: "I have done / As you have done—that's what I can; induced / As you have been—that's for my country" (1.9.15–17). But a citizen rightfully questions his claim to the consulship: "You have deserved nobly of your country and you have not deserved nobly" (2.3.84–85). When Coriolanus sarcastically seeks clarification of his "enigma" (2.3.86), the citizen explains: "You have been a scourge to her enemies, you have been a rod to her friends; you have not indeed loved the common people" (2.3.87–89). It will also be recalled that Mark Antony called Brutus "the noblest Roman of them all" (*JC* 5.5.68) because "He only, in a general honest thought / And *common good to all,* made one of them" (5.5.71–72, emphasis added).

Coriolanus's flaw in nobility is his proud contempt for the citizens of Rome. It is dramatized when, contrary to Plutarch, he balks at putting on the garment of humility, asking for the people's "voices" (2.2.138), and showing them his wounds. "Must I," he complains, "With my base tongue give to my noble heart / A lie that it must bear?" (3.2.99–101). This statement is flawed in the sense of excessive nobility. Most of the treatises describing true nobility deplore this haughty conduct, the very kind that Coriolanus exhibits when he is presented for consul. Roger Ascham, for example, lists in 1570 "stoute wilfulness" as one of the "two greatest enemies to nobilitie."[5] Sir Thomas Elyot exclaims, "Lord God, how they be blinded which do wene that haulte countenance is a comelyness of nobilitie."[6] Most other authorities urge that noblemen be adaptable, even "common" in relations with the citizens: according to Lawrence Humphrey, "Towards the multitude eke, and common sort, some duties must bee observed: that Nobilitie maye (as it were) flow into all mens hertes."[7] And James Cleland, in a statement that helps to clarify Menenius's "too noble for the world," advises noblemen: "It is great wisdom for a man to accommodate himself and to frame his manners apt and meete for al honest conference, and society of men . . . . It is a most rare quality in a Noble man to be common, that maketh him imitate Gods goodness."[8] Coriolanus's friends urge him to apologize to the people and the tribunes. As a Herculean hero he is magnificent in defying the tribunes' threats and in choosing "Death on the wheel or at wild horses' heels" (3.2.2). The reaction of the wiser sort, however, is one of admiration mixed with doubt, as hinted at by the unenthusiastic response by one patrician, "You do the nobler" (3.2.6). His mother's opinion is clearer: "You are too absolute, / Though therein you can never be too noble, / But when extremities speak" (3.2.39–41). But she hints, without full awareness of her own role, at what has made extremities in her son and caused his banishment: "You might have been enough the man you are, / With striving less to be so" (3.2.19–20).

And as she had been responsible for his trying too hard to be a man on this occasion, so her influence will prove mortal, as he foresees, when he leaves his country to lead the Volscian forces against Rome.

Soldier and Society

Early in the play the fable of the Belly and its Members accurately places Coriolanus as "the arm our soldier" (1.1.111). The soldier was a dangerous, troublesome, but necessary member of society. Shakespeare makes his early and complete dedication to war a reason that he cannot behave civilly in peace. The problem of the soldier in society was a source of much concern in England, and it was good capital for conflict in literary works, of which *Coriolanus* is the supreme example.

Shakespeare, in drawing his hero as one "bred i'th' wars" (3.1.319), was relying upon popular knowledge of the unlucky civil careers of Elizabethan commanders, conspicuously Essex and his military friends, members of the "war party"—men, to use Bacon's words, of a "military dependence." Bacon's letter of warning to the Earl might well, in large part, have been addressed to Shakespeare's hero. Essex is rebuked principally for being "of a nature not to be ruled." Another serious fault, carefully analyzed by Bacon, is

that of a military dependence. Wherein I cannot sufficiently wonder at your Lordship's course; that you say, the wars are your occupation, and go on in that course; whereas, if I might have advised your Lordship, you should have left that person at Plymouth; more than when in council . . . it had been in season.[9]

In his arrogant confidence, Coriolanus is a hazard when he speaks of peace or war. In his stalwart resistance to the people's case, at his trial, he wonders that his mother

> Does not approve me further, who was wont
> To call them wooden vessals, things created
> To buy and sell with groats, to show bare heads
> In congregations, to yawn, be still and wonder,
> When one but of my ordinance stood up
> To speak of peace or war.
>
> (3.2.8–13)

His questionable wisdom in speaking "of peace or war" in social problems had earlier been demonstrated when he offered a warrior's solution to the popular riots:

> They say there's grain enough?
> Would the nobility lay aside their ruth,

> And let me use my sword, I'd make a quarry
> With thousands of these quartered slaves as high
> As I could pick my lance.
>
> (1.1.191–95)

He has the war party's cruel philosophy that war can heal social wounds. It was believed by many that this party instigated war to get rid of excess (and disrupting) common people. Marcius is of this conviction when he hears that "the Voices are in arms" (1.1.219). He is pleased at the news: "I am glad on't. Then we shall ha' means to vent / Our musty superfluity" (1.2.220–21).

We need not be surprised, accordingly, that in times of peace the government banished its military defenders. Lord Burlegh wrote to his son advising against the military as a career: "it is a science no longer in request than in use: soldiers in peace are like chimneys in summer."[10] Soldier-authors like Barnabe Riche never tired of stories showing the noble warrior ill-used by the society he has served. The usual recourse of the society was banishment. Shortly before he wrote *Coriolanus*, we recall, Shakespeare had depicted in *Timon* the plight and subsequent reverse of a captain ill-used and then banished by the senate. In a long diatribe, of which the following is small part, Alcibiades attacks the ungrateful "usurers":

> I'm worse than mad: I have kept back their foes
> While they have told their money and let out
> Their coin upon large interest, I myself
> Rich only in large hurts. All those for this?
> Is this the balsam that the usuring senate
> Pours into captain's wounds? Banishment!
> It comes not ill; I hate not to be banished;
> It is a cause worthy my spleen and fury,
> That I may strike at Athens.
>
> (*Tim* 3.5.105–113)

Here, as almost everywhere in similar situations, banishment is as dangerous as harboring military malcontents in peace. The exiled warrior will lead an army against his hated country.

So it is with Coriolanus. And he adds the threat that now Rome will be without defenders. "I banish you!" (3.3.124) he cries to the "common cry of curs" (3.3.121).

Let every feeble rumor shake your hearts!
Your enemies, with nodding of their plumes,
Fan you into despair! Have the power still
To banish your defenders, till at length
Your ignorance—which finds not till it feels,
Making but reservation of yourselves,
Still your own foes—deliver you as most
Abated captives to some nation
That won you without blows! Despising,
For you, the city, thus I turn my back.
There is a world elsewhere.

(3.3.126–136)

The naive plebs rejoice at their "victory." "The people's enemy is gone, is gone!" (3.3.137). "Our enemy is banished! he is gone!" (3.3.138). And, according to the stage directions, "They all shout, and throw up their hats."

Coriolanus, with fire in his mind, thus turns to a "world elsewhere." But though this world will be with his former enemies, Antium and Tullus Aufidius, who are now to be allies, it is essentially the same world, the only world that the warrior has known. Aufidius receives him gladly, as one in joint commission against "the bowels of ungrateful Rome" (4.5.131). Burning all resistance (where there is any) en route, the army makes its way almost to the gates of Rome.

But then, after a long series of acts centering on curses, riots, furious trials, and revengeful war, Shakespeare's sense of pace, helped by his dramatic versatility, again creates a miracle. The rest of the play turns from suffering as wrath to suffering as humanity. The language, metallic and cold from the beginning, becomes correspondingly lyrical and beautiful. And these changes are highlighted in a scene as dramatic and tender as Shakespeare (helped by Plutarch) ever wrote: the intercession of the women.

Toward a Humane Nobility

While Coriolanus is, unknowingly to the people, making his terrible approach toward Rome, the complacent citizens and tribunes are rejoicing at their unaccustomed harmony. Sicinius proudly reports his accomplishments:

> We hear not of him, neither need we fear him;
> His remedies are tame: the present peace
> And quietness of the people, which before
> Were in wild hurry.
>
> (4.6.1–4)

But soon a messenger arrives with the shocking news. Unless Coriolanus shows mercy, Rome will be burned. Two of the general's best friends have been sent pleading to the Volscian camp, only to be rejected. Menenius, confident of his friend's love, and then heartbroken at his coldness, tells the Romans that "there is no more mercy in him than there is milk in a male tiger" (5.4.27–28). He has no hope that the last Roman recourse, sending Volumnia, Virgilia, Valeria, and his son, will have any effect. Shakespeare prepares the scene effectively for their appearance by having Menenius describe in more detail Coriolanus's total lack of feeling for any of those he once loved. The coldness of his manner, and the metallic way it is described, harks back to his earlier manner. When Sicinius protests, "He loved his mother dearly" (5.4.15), Menenius counters:

So did he me; and he no more remembers his mother now than an eight-year-old horse. The tartness of his face sours ripe grapes. When he walks, he moves like an engine, and the ground shrinks before his treading. He is able to pierce a corslet with his eye; talks like a knell and his hum is a battery. (5.4.16–21)

Menenius is proved utterly wrong. For the first time we see a Coriolanus torn by inner strife and suffering as a fallible human being. When the ladies enter, he is deeply shaken, but he tries to resist natural impulses that until now he has too nobly controlled:

> My wife comes foremost; then the honored mould
> Wherein this trunk was framed, and in her hand
> The grandchild to her blood. But out, affection!
> All bond and privilege of nature, break!
> Let it be virtuous to be obstinate.
> What is that curt'sy worth? or those doves' eyes,
> Which can make gods forswarn? I melt, and am not
> Of stronger earth than others.
>
> (5.3.22–29)

Still he resists the cry of "great nature" (5.3.33) and resolves to stand "As if a man were author of himself / And knew no other kin"

(5.3.36–37). Few characters in Shakespeare can speak with such feeling eloquence, or suffer so from equal loyalties. His family kneels to him, but he tries to harden himself. Shakespeare gives him the simile that was one of the dramatist's most intuitive favorites:

> Like a dull actor now,
> I have forgot my part, and I am out,
> Even to a full disgrace. Best of my flesh,
> Forgive my tyranny; but do not say
> For that, "Forgive our Romans." O, a kiss
> Long as my exile, sweet as my revenge!
> Now, by the jealous queen of heaven, that kiss
> I carried from thee dear; and my true lip
> Hath virgined it e'er since.
>
> (5.3.40–48)

Mainly it is his mother who now will speak, and she does so with both her patrician eloquence and her assured knowledge of his love. She reminds him of the supplicants' dilemma, their inability to pray for both him and Rome. She doubtless gains emotion from her warning him of how history will record his loss of patriotic nobility:

> "The man was noble,
> But with his last attempt he wiped it out,
> Destroyed his country; and his name remains
> To th' ensuing age abhorred."
>
> (5.3.145–48)

And still on the virtue that once meant most to him: "Why dost not speak? / Think'st thou it honorable for a noble man / Still to remember wrongs?" (5.3.153–55).

But Coriolanus is now moved more by human impulses, by affection, "bond and privilege of nature" (5.3.25). And the brief conclusion of her long plea is worth all the rest:

> Come, let us go.
> This fellow had a Volscian to his mother;
> His wife is in Corioles, and this child
> Like him by chance.
>
> (5.3.177–80)

There are uncanny times in Shakespeare when, whatever his verbal resources, silence is best. This is such a time, and Shakespeare makes

it unmistakable in the stage direction: "holds her by the hand silent."
Adding to the poignancy of the union is the foreshadowed parting.
The two will never meet again, nor will he again see young Marcius
or his wife. For he knows something that his sterner mother does not
think of: his sacrifice for Rome and family will be total:

> O my mother, mother! O!
> You have won a happy victory to Rome;
> But for your son—believe it, O believe it—
> Most dangerously you have with him prevailed,
> If not most mortal to him.
>
> (5.3.185–89)

We must note that he weeps, as well as concedes, for Aufidius is critically and coolly watching the scene, knowing that he can use it back
in Antium to disgrace and kill the warrior whom he now hates.

Before he left Rome, Coriolanus assured his mother of two things.
The first is a promise he carries out:

> Though I go alone,
> Like to a lonely dragon, though his fen
> Makes feared and talked of more than seen—your son
> Will or exceed the common or be caught
> With cautelous baits and practice.
>
> (4.1.29–33)

He will prove himself above the "common"—that is, will be noble—
or, if destroyed, be so by base means—as a noble warrior still. And
so it in fact happens when he tries to present himself to the Volscian
nobility as victorious but is forestalled by Aufidius. The Volscian
leader, many times unable to defeat the Roman in fair fight, had re-
solved to "potch" (1.10.15) at him, "or wrath or craft will get him"
(1.10.16). It now will be craft, for he has hired conspirators to second
his accusations with swords. The first accusation is the intolerable
"traitor" (5.6.84). The second is that Coriolanus (now Marcius to
him) had given up "for certain drops of salt, your city Rome"
(5.6.92). There follows the cruelest of travesty of what for Coriolanus
had been an act of filial love: "at his nurse's tears / He whined and
roared away your victory" (5.6.96–97). Coriolanus, once more as in
Rome moved to wrathful indiscretion, begins, "Hear'st thou, Mars?"
(5.6.99). But Aufidius goads him still further by "Name not the
god, thou boy of tears!" (5.6.100). "Boy" was not only one of the
most insulting Elizabethan epithets, but, for Coriolanus, no word

could more deeply expose his somewhat unusual attachment to his mother. Once more moved "to choler straight" (3.3.25), as the Roman tribune had advised the people to render Coriolanus, the disgraced warrior virtually reenacts his trial and outbreak in Rome, even to the screams of the people. But now he is shamefully slain by conspirators and stood upon by Aufidius. The noble are noble in Corioli as in Rome, and they had tried to prevent "a deed whereat valor will weep" (5.6.131). The best they can do is to assure him a noble memory and noble rites.

His fealty to his second promise is harder to assess: "While I remain above the ground, you shall / Hear from me still, and never of me aught / But what is like me formerly" (4.1.51–53). Although he tries to remain noble to a new country ("No more infected with my [former] country's love / Than when I parted hence," 5.6.72–73), his mother predicts that if he destroys Rome his name will remain "To th' ensuing age abhorred." He will, however, be still his stalwart self, true to his own sense of constancy and nobility. In the Volscian camp he advises his son in words that have characterized him before and will still, despite a passionate move, characterize him forever uniquely and best:

> The god of soldiers,
> With the consent of supreme Jove, inform
> Thy thoughts with nobleness, that thou may'st prove
> To shame invulnerable, and stick i'th' wars
> Like a great sea-mark, standing every flaw
> And saving those that eye thee.

> (5.3.71–76)

And even a Volscian Lord pronounces: "Let him be regarded / As the most noble corse that ever herald / Did follow to his urn" (5.6.141–43).

The stark power of this tragedy, as well as its rugged beauty, has been captured in music by the composer most adequate to heroic passions, Beethoven. He does so in his *Coriolan* overture (opus 62, 1807) for "a tragedy after Shakespeare" by Heinrich von Collin, but his major inspiration was, according to Ernest Brennecke,[11] doubtless Shakespeare. And the powerful opening chords suggest his understanding of the play. The overture, heard after a reading of the tragedy, not only heightens and makes tolerable the tragic experience; it brings together two masters of music—verbal and orchestral.

Chapter Twelve

Conclusion

To conclude a book on Shakespeare's tragedies leaves the author with mixed feelings. Abandoning—so far as one can abandon—a sustained period of the highest level of feeling is a relief, if not a necessity. One cannot live forever with the intensity that tragic poetry demands. Nor is it without peril to leave a necessarily ordinary view of life. Such a view is sometimes as welcome as that of the clownish Porter after the murder of Duncan. Following the prolonged learning and living experience that comes from acquaintance with a Hamlet, a Lear, a Cleopatra, or a Macbeth must come the levelness of life that keeps one safely sane. And, though all bright things must fade, the inevitability of death to these lordly creatures is a challenge to us. True, most of them die into greatness. But at present it seems almost attractive to sit down to a book on survival in Shakespearean tragedy: to study rationally, but not upliftingly, men like Octavius Caesar, Malcolm, and Horatio, or women like Octavia.

But death is not—unless it grips our hearts by the loss of others—the be-all and the end-all of Shakespearean tragedy. And this assertion brings us to the necessity that makes finishing the book less than a total pleasure. For we must at least privately guess at the worth of the hypothesis that inaugurated the study. Worth, rather than correctness: for the rightness or wrongness of these guidelines would be more appropriate for a scientific treatise. Every book on tragic poetry must be venturesomely written, with results as surprising to the author as they may be appalling to the reader.

But let us try. And let us hope that the reader has not felt the heavy hand of a thesis: not even the hypothesis that Shakespeare's tragedies are greater than plot or event or death. And, at least in this respect, the emotional experience of writing about the plays has vindicated what we have proposed: that the ordeal, the feeling, the passion is what controls us during the tragedies and what will bind us to them. We will remember the bustling of accidents and casual events attending the death of Hamlet; but we are more likely to suffer repeatedly with him through his earlier perplexities and heartache. If event or death were paramount, how could we share the passion of a Lady Macbeth, a Coriolanus, or a Timon?

The stress upon humanity, the other major hypothesis, need not be justified only by what the Renaissance would most anxiously have needed. Uniquely versed in all kinds of individuals, Shakespeare unassisted would have known their separate but somehow common need for the reassurance of civilized and humane behavior. All Elizabethans would have felt the desolation of a Macbeth in losing that which must accompany more than old age: "As honor, love, obedience, troops of friends" (*Mac* 5.3.25). And they would have been well acquainted with other virtues of humanity as well, including nobility and loyalty. Some readers will not agree with the proposal that the concern for humanity should make us ashamed of the eager vindictiveness we feel for the torture of an Aaron or an Iago. Such readers, in fact, may be closer to Shakespeare the popular dramatist who wisely let the audience respond, with relief, to its pent-up emotions, even as in a more favorable sense, to the need for comic relief in *Macbeth*.

A serious misgiving that every author has upon completing a book is a sense of omission. A book could be, and indeed several have been, written on Shakespeare's language. More could have been said even here upon the improvements in dramatic language that *Antony* achieves over *Romeo*. But it will be hoped that attention has been paid to the increasing individualization of verse and prose style even as, on the whole, the tendency is toward more irregular power (as in *Lear*) and less lyricism (as in *Romeo*). And we have noticed the uncanny change from a harshly powerful language in Coriolanus to his gentle poetry of sacrificial love in his last scene with his mother.

It is more constructive, however, to subordinate partial omission in favor of what is suggested for future studies in Shakespeare's tragedies. One major prospect has appeared from the writing of this book, and that is its feminine point of view. We can credit ourselves with at least calling attention to what cannot escape attention: the powerful women in three of the last tragedies. But current scholarship is going well beyond such obviousness. It is as though, through translation, Shakespeare had become available to a whole country. But this endeavor is even more sweeping. A half of humanity is being included in a world of women, created by a dramatist who rewards the fullest study of all humanity. In the feminist "revolution," for example, the tragedy of *King Lear* can be studied by daughters rather than fathers. And a truer, even more disconcerting view of sexuality in *Othello* is now emerging from the insights of female scholars.[1]

The above reflections, however, mainly make it obvious that a book on Shakespeare's tragedies cannot be concluded. And the conclusion cannot be written because a Shakespearean tragedy cannot be concluded. These works may have endings, most commonly the restitution of the state. But how can one conclude to his satisfaction *King Lear*? We will be forever haunted by Lear's final words: "Do you see this? Look on her! Look her lips, / Look there, look there—" (*Lear* 5.3.311–12). Here are directions toward a future that, during our mortal lives, we will forever strive to see. Simple lines, they yet—to quote Arnold's sonnet "Shakespeare"—outtop knowledge.

And then there are the questions, great abiding questions, that serve to make Shakespeare's tragedies open-ended. We begin with the excited discovery of a thirteen-year-old girl, Juliet: "What's in a name?" (*RJ* 2.2.43). In the answer to this question we might find the answer to the rifts of mankind. But Shakespeare, to quote Arnold again, will not abide our question. Then we turn to *Hamlet* and *the* question of "To be, or not to be" (*Ham* 3.1.56). Nor should we neglect, as is usually done, the bleak existential question of the play's first line, "Who's there?" (*Ham* 1.1.1). Characteristically, as in *Romeo and Juliet*, Shakespeare will place the motif of a play in the form of a question. In *Othello* it is a question that probably Shakespeare himself could not answer. It is Othello's "Will you, I pray, demand that demi-devil / Why he hath thus ensnared my soul and body?" (*Oth* 5.2.300–1). *King Lear* is full of questions that underlie all mankind's perplexities and philosophies. One need not be a king to ask, in utter human loneliness, "Does any here know me?" (*Lear* 1.4.216) or in utter cosmic loneliness, similar to "Who's there?": "Who is it that can tell me who I am?" (*Lear* 1.4.220). But one must have been driven mad by stony inhumanity to ask, "Is there any cause in nature that makes these hard hearts?" (*Lear* 3.6.75–76). Finally, because we have scored a zero on all these questions, we turn to one in *Macbeth* to which a modern authority has given a wise, but not comforting answer. Macbeth, thinking as much of himself as of his wife, asks the doctor:

> Canst thou not minister to a mind diseased,
> Pluck from the memory a rooted sorrow,
> Raze out the written troubles of the brain,
> And with some sweet oblivious antidote
> Cleanse the stuffed bosom of that perilous stuff
> Which weighs upon the heart?
>
> (*Mac* 5.3.40–45)

"Over the centuries," writes Alfred Harbage,[2] "comes the quiet answer, convincing us, as so often the words of this poet do, that nothing further can be said, 'Therein the patient / Must minister to himself' [*Mac* 5.3.45–46]."

Last of all, allied to the archetypal questions, are the great passages that come back to us, unexpectedly and with what Emerson called "an alienated majesty":[3] for they embody our own thoughts, thoughts that do not really become ours until we see them in Shakespeare's verse. Moreover, much of Shakespeare is for us an aftershock. There are lines meaningless to us when we first read them. Only when we have become through education in life worthy of them do they "return" to us. These are passages like Lear's "O reason not the need" (*Lear* 2.4.259) or Othello's "Farewell" (*Oth* 3.3.348) or "Put out the light" (*Oth* 5.2.7). They need not even have a substantial content of thought. A critic once remarked that one line always brought tears to his eyes, Hamlet's "Nay, but to live / In the rank sweat of an enseamed bed" (*Ham* 3.4.92–93). Another, chosen as a "touchstone" by Matthew Arnold, is Hamlet's simple line, but a line connoting the entire play: "Absent thee from felicity awhile" (*Ham* 5.2.336). One need not even fully understand the haunting words and images, as in Antony's words of desolation:

> All come to this? The hearts
> That spanieled me at heels, to whom I gave
> Their wishes, do discandy, melt their sweets
> On blossoming Caesar; and this pine is barked
> That overtopped them all.
>
> (*AC* 4.12.20–24)

It is, in short, to disparage Shakespeare if we hope to "conclude" a tragedy. As we grow older, as our loss changes from a Juliet to a Cordelia, Shakespeare's tragedies will come back to us—misquoted perhaps—at needed moments. Like Prospero, Shakespeare taught us language, and our "profit on't" (*Tem* 1.2.363) is that what is unconscious has become conscious, and what is conscious has become articulate.

Notes and References

Preface

1. Joseph Conrad, preface to *The Nigger of the Narcissus,* in *Typhoon and Other Tales* (New York: Signet Classics, 1962), 21.

Chapter One

1. References to Christopher Marlowe are to *The Complete Plays,* ed. Irving Ribner (New York: Odyssey Press, 1963).
2. Reuben A. Brower, *Hero & Saint: Shakespeare and the Graeco-Roman Heroic Tradition* (New York and Oxford, 1971), 29–83.
3. George Chapman, *Chapman's Homer,* ed. Allardyce Nicoll (Princeton: Princeton University Press, 1956), 1:23.
4. Sir Thomas Smith, *De Republica Anglorum* (London, 1583), 4.
5. Emanuel van Meteren, *History of the Netherlands* (1599), in W. B. Rye, *England As Seen by Foreigners* (London, 1865), 70.
6. In James Spedding, *The Letters and Life of Francis Bacon* (London, 1862), 2:413.
7. Jan van Linschoten, *The Fight and Cyclone at Azores,* in Arber's English Reprints (London, 1871), 91–92.
8. Fulke Greville, *Life of Sir Philip Sidney* (1652; reprint, Oxford: Clarendon Press, 1907), 33.
9. Quoted by C. S. Lewis in *English Literature in the Sixteenth Century* (Oxford: Clarendon Press, 1954), 346–47.
10. Machiavelli, *The Prince,* trans. Robert M. Adams (New York: Norton, 1977), 50.
11. Boethius, *Consolation of Philosophy,* trans. George Colville (1556), ed. Ernest Belfort Bax (London, 1897), 51.
12. Virgil, *The Aeneid,* trans. H. Rushton Fairclough (Cambridge: Harvard University Press, ca. 1935). 272–73.
13. Augustine, *The City of God,* trans. John Healey, ed. R. V. G. Tasker (London: Dent, 1962), book 14, chapter 9.
14. Cicero, *Tusculan Disputations,* ed. T. E. Page et al., trans. J. E. King (Cambridge: Harvard University Press, 1945), 239–41.
15. M. J. Abernethy, *A Christian and Heavenly Treatise* (London, 1630), 236.
16. John Donne, *Sermons,* ed. G. R. Potter and Evelyn Simpson (Berkeley and Los Angeles: University of California Press, 1953–62), 4:172.
17. Edward Topsell, *Times Lamentation* (London, 1599), 3.
18. William Perkins, *Cases of Conscience* (London, 1608), 99.

19. Ephraim Huit, *The Anatomy of Conscience* (London, 1626), 107.

20. Gervase Babington, *Comfortable Notes on Genesis* (London, 1602), 16.

21. Jeremiah Dyke, *Good Conscience* (London, 1624), 42.

22. Richard Hooker, *Of the Laws of Ecclesiastical Polity* (The First Book) (London: Dent, 1954), 157.

23. Sir Thomas Elyot, *The Governor* (London: Dent, 1937), 3.

24. "An Exhortacion Concerning Good Order and Obedience to Rulers and Magistrate," in *Sixteenth-Century Prose,* ed. Karl J. Holzknecht (New York: Harper, 1954), 123.

25. Richard Sewell, "The Tragic Form," *Essays in Criticism* 4 (October 1954):345.

26. A. P. Rossiter, "Shakespearian Tragedy," in *Angel with Horns and Other Shakespeare Lectures,* ed. Graham Storey (London: Longman's, 1961), 263.

Chapter Two

1. Eugene Waith, "The Metamorphosis of Violence in *Titus Andronicus,*" *Shakespeare Survey* 10 (1957): 39–49.

2. Hereward Price, "Mirror-Scenes in Shakespeare," in *Joseph Quincy Adams Memorial Studies,* ed. James G. McManaway, Giles E. Dawson, and Edwin E. Willoughby (Washington, D.C.: Folger Shakespeare Library, 1948), 101–13.

3. Matthew Arnold, "Shakespeare," in *Arnold Poetical Works,* ed. C. B. Tinker and H. F. Lowry (London: Oxford University Press, 1969), 2–3.

Chapter Three

1. Caroline Spurgeon, *Shakespeare's Imagery and What It Tells Us* (Cambridge: Cambridge University Press, 1935), 310–16.

2. Bertrand Evans, "The Brevity of Friar Laurence," *PMLA* 65 (September 1950): 841–65.

3. *Augustine: Earlier Writings,* trans. John H. S. Burleigh (Philadelphia: The Westminster Press, n.d.), 211. See also John Calvin's 100th Sermon on the Book of Job, in *Sermons on the Book of Job,* trans. Arthur Golding (London, 1574), 469 b 45: "Thus, then ye see why our Lord doth expressly threaten the wicked, to punish them even in their children. It is to the ende that wee shoulde bee touched neerer the quicke with feare, seeing that men are so dull and hardhearted of their owne nature."

4. *Spenser's Poetical Works,* ed. J. C. Smith and E. De Selincourt (London: Oxford University Press, 1966), 2.28.29.

Chapter Four

1. S. F. Johnson, ed., introduction to *Julius Caesar* in *William Shakespeare: The Complete Works,* Pelican Text. Revised, ed. Alfred Harbage (New York, 1977), 897.

2. A recent scholarly argument has centered upon Brutus's insensitivity as a Stoic. Critics adverse to Brutus are John Anson in *"Julius Caesar:* The Politics of the Hardened Heart," *Shakespeare Studies* 2 (1966): 11–33, and Marvin L. Vawter, " 'Division 'tween Our Souls': Shakespeare's Stoic Brutus," *Shakespeare Studies* 7 (1974): 173–95. Defending Brutus as a humane Stoic is Ruth M. Levitsky, "The Elements Were So Mix'd . . . ," *PMLA* 88 (March 1973): 240–45.

3. The ritualizing of brutality in the play is ably discussed by Brents Stirling in *Unity in Shakespearian Tragedy: The Interplay of Theme and Character.* (New York, 1956), chap. 4, pp. 40–54.

4. Renaissance works arguing the merits and demerits of Stoicism include Thomas Rogers, *A Philosophical Discourse Entituled, The Anatomie of the Minde* (London, 1576); Justus Lipsius, *Two Books of Constancie,* trans. Sir John Stradling (London, 1594); and Guillaume du Vair, *The Moral Philosophie of the Stoicks,* trans. Thomas James (London, 1598).

Chapter Five

1. William Hazlitt, *Characters of Shakespeare's Plays* (London, 1817) in *Shakespeare Criticism:* A Selection, ed. D. Nicol Smith (London: Oxford University Press, 1944), 323.

2. Samuel Taylor Coleridge, *Table Talk* in *Coleridge's Writings on Shakespeare,* ed. Terence Hawkes (New York: Capricorn Books, 1959), 140.

3. G. Wilson Knight, "The Embassy of Death: An Essay on *Hamlet,"* in *The Wheel of Fire: Interpretation of Shakespeare's Tragedy* (Cleveland and New York: The World Publishing Co., 1963), chap. 2, pp. 17–46.

4. Caroline Spurgeon, *Shakespeare's Imagery,* 316–20.

5. Barnabe Riche, *Allarme to England* (London, 1578), signature B4^v.

6. Lancelot Dawes, *Gods Mercies and Jerusalems Miseries,* (London, 1609), signature A4^r.

7. Thomas Lodge and Robert Greene, *A Looking-Glass for London and England,* ed. W. W. Greg (Oxford, 1932), lines 1990–96.

8. Fredson Bowers, "Hamlet as Minister and Scourge," *PMLA* 70 (September 1955): 740–49.

Chapter Six

1. Bernard Spivack, *Shakespeare and the Allegory of Evil: The History of the Metaphor in Relation to His Major Villains* (New York, 1958). For Iago, see particularly chapters one, two, and twelve.

2. Leah Scragg, "Iago—Vice or Devil?" *Shakespeare Survey* 21 (1969):53–65.

3. T. S. Eliot, "Shakespeare and the Stoicism of Seneca," in *Selected Essays of T. S. Eliot,* 3d rev. ed. (London: Faber and Faber, 1951), 130–31.

Chapter Seven

1. John Keats, "On Sitting Down to Read *King Lear* Once Again," in *The Poetical Works of John Keats,* ed. H. Buxton Forman (London: Oxford University Press, 1929), 302–3.

2. Samuel Johnson, *Johnson on Shakespeare,* ed. Walter Raleigh (London: Oxford University Press, 1949), 161–62.

3. Charles Lamb, "On Shakespeare's Tragedies" (1808), in *The Complete Works in Prose and Verse of Charles Lamb* (London: Chatto & Windus, 1875), 261.

4. Samuel Taylor Coleridge, *Lectures and Notes on Shakespeare* (1818), collected by T. Ashe (London: George Bell and Sons, 1890), 341.

5. A. C. Swinburne, *A Study of Shakespeare* (1876; reprint, London: Chatto & Windus, 1902), 173.

6. Hazlitt, *Characters of Shakespeare's Plays,* 328.

7. Thomas Norton and Thomas Sackville, *Gorboduc,* in *Five Elizabethan Tragedies,* ed. A. K. McIlwraith (London: Oxford University Press, 1957), 69–129; cited in text by act, scene, and line.

8. Hooker, *Laws of Ecclesiastical Polity,* 157.

Chapter Eight

1. Thomas De Quincey, *On the Knocking at the Gate in "Macbeth"* (1823), in *Shakespeare Criticism,* ed. D. Nicol Smith, 374–75.

2. L. C. Knights, *Explorations* (1946; reprint, London: Chatto and Windus, 1951), 18–19.

3. Nicholas Remy, *Demonaltry,* trans. E. A. Ashwin, ed. Rev. Montague Summers (London: J. Rodker, 1930), 108.

4. Walter Clyde Curry, *Shakespeare's Philosophical Patterns* (1937; rpt. Baton Rouge: University of Louisiana Press, 1959), 43.

5. Glynne Wickham, "Hell-Castle and Its Door-Keeper," *Shakespeare Survey* 19 (1966): 68–69, 73.

6. Thomas De Quincey, *On the Knocking,* 378. (See chap. 8, note 1.)

7. George Meredith, "Lucifer in Starlight" (1883), in *The Poems of George Meredith,* ed. Phyllis B. Bartlett (New Haven and London: Yale University Press, 1978), 1:285.

Chapter Nine

1. Samuel Taylor Coleridge, *Coleridge's Shakespearean Criticism,* ed. T. M. Raysor (London: Constable & Co., 1930), 1:238.

2. G. Wilson Knight, "The Pilgrimage of Hate," in *The Wheel of Fire,* 220–21.

3. Rolf Soellner, *"Timon of Athens": Shakespeare's Pessimistic Tragedy* (Columbus, Ohio, 1979).

4. O. J. Campbell, *Shakespeare's Satire* (London: Oxford University Press, 1943), 185–92.

5. J. M. Nosworthy, *Shakespeare's Occasional Plays* (London: Arnold, 1965), 45, 225–26.

6. Willard Farnham, *Shakespeare's Tragic Frontier: The World of His Final Tragedies* (Berkeley and Los Angeles, 1950). See particularly chapter two, 39–77.

7. Reprinted and translated from the Italian version of N. da Lonigo (1536) by Geoffrey Bullough in *Narrative and Dramatic Sources of Shakespeare* (London: Routledge and Kegan Paul, 1966), 6:263–77.

8. *Euphues,* in *The Complete Works of John Lyly,* ed. R. Warwick Bond (Oxford: Clarendon, 1902), 1:218.

9. Dedication to *Volpone,* in *The Complete Plays of Ben Jonson* (London: Dent, n.d.), 1:401.

Chapter Ten

1. G. Wilson Knight, "The Transcendental Humanism of Antony and Cleopatra," in *The Imperial Theme* (London: Methuen & Co., 1951), 210.

2. Madeleine Doran, "High Events as These: The Language of Hyperbole in *Antony and Cleopatra,*" in *Shakespeare's Dramatic Language* (Madison: The University of Wisconsin Press, 1976), 155.

3. Linda Fitz [Woodbridge], "Egyptian Queens and Male Reviewers: Sexist Attitudes in *Antony and Cleopatra* Criticism," *Shakespeare Quarterly* 28 (Summer 1977): 297–316.

4. *Coleridge's Writings on Shakespeare,* ed. Terence Hawkes (New York: Capricorn Books, 1959), 245.

5. G. Bernard Shaw, "Better Than Shakespear?" in *Shaw on Shakespeare,* ed. Edwin Wilson (New York: Dutton, 1961), 213.

6. Matthew N. Proser, *"Antony and Cleopatra:* The Heroic Image," in *The Heroic Image in Five Shakespearean Tragedies* (Princeton, 1965), 171–235.

7. Maurice Charney, *Shakespeare's Roman Plays: The Function of Imagery in the Drama* (Cambridge, 1961), 131.

8. Maynard Mack, ed., introduction to *Antony and Cleopatra* in *William Shakespeare,* ed. Harbage, 1171. The George Meredith sonnet is number fifty from *Modern Love* (1862).

Chapter Eleven

1. Osorio da Fonseca, *The Five Bookes of Civill and Christian Nobilities,* trans. William Blandie (London, 1576), sig. B 2ʳ.

2. Harry Levin, ed., introduction to *Coriolanus* in *William Shakespeare,* ed. Harbage, 1212.

3. Geoffrey Bullough, ed., *Narrative and Dramatic Sources of Shakespeare* (London: Routledge and Kegan Paul, 1964), 5:458.

4. Henry Peacham, *The Compleat Gentleman* (London: 1634; reprint, Oxford: Oxford University Press, 1906), 2.

5. Roger Ascham, *The Scholemaster,* ed. William Aldis Wright (Cambridge: Cambridge University Press, 1904), 206.

6. Sir Thomas Elyot, *The Governor,* 13–31.

7. Lawrence Humphrey, *The Nobles or of Nobilitye* (London, 1563), signature N6ᵛ.

8. James Cleland, *The Institution of a Young Noble Man* (London, 1607), 168–69.

9. Bacon to the earl of Essex, 4 October 1596 in James Spedding, *The Letters and Life,* 2:413.

10. Lord Burlegh, in *Annals of the Reformation,* ed. John Strype (Oxford: Oxford University Press), 4:477.

11. Ernest Brennecke, "Music Based on Shakespeare," in *The Reader's Encyclopedia of Shakespeare,* ed. Oscar James Campbell and Edward G. Quinn (New York: Thomas Y. Crowell Co., 1966), 572.

Chapter Twelve

1. As an exploratory essay to her projected book on *Othello* as a tragedy of sexuality, Lynda E. Boose has published "Othello's Handkerchief: 'The Recognizance and Pledge of Love,' " *English Literary Renaissance* 5 (Autumn 1975):360–74.

2. Alfred Harbage, ed., introduction to *William Shakespeare,* 1109.

3. Ralph Waldo Emerson, "Self-Reliance," in *Essays* (London: Dent, 1938), 30.

Selected Bibliography

PRIMARY SOURCES

These sources consist of the First Folio, 1623, in which about half of all the plays appeared for the first time, and various quartos. The quartos are copies of individual plays, published mainly during Shakespeare's lifetime. Some of these are "bad quartos"—garbled, mislineated, and incomplete—due to pirating, careless composition, stenographic reporting, memorial reconstruction, or imperfect copies. Most, however, are of good quality. Modern editions are based upon quartos (if they exist for the play) and the First Folio. Titles from the First Folio are head-titles.

The Tragedie of Anthonie, and Cleopatra. First Folio, 1623.

The Tragedy of Coriolanus. First Folio, 1623.

The Tragicall Historie of Hamlet Prince of Denmark. By William Shakespeare. As it hath been diverse times acted by his Highnesse servants in the Cittie of London: as also in the two Universities of Cambridge and Oxford, and else-where. First Quarto, 1603. A "bad quarto."

The Tragicall Historie of Hamlet, Prince of Denmarke. By William Shakespeare. Newly imprinted and enlarged to almost as much againe as it was, according to the true and perfect Coppie. Second Quarto, 1604.

The Tragedie of Hamlet, Prince of Denmarke. First Folio, 1623.

The Tragedie of Julius Caesar. First Folio, 1623.

M. William Shak-speare: His True Chronicle Historie of the life and death of King Lear and his three Daughters. With the unfortunate life of Edgar, sonne and heire to the Earle of Gloster, and his sullen and assumed humor of Tom of Bedlam: As it was played before the Kings Majestie at Whitehall upon S. Stephans night in Christmas Hollidays. By his Majesties servants playing usually at the Gloabe on the Bancke-side. First Quarto, 1608. [Second quarto has essentially the same title. Dated 1608 on the title page, it was actually published in 1619].

The Tragedie of King Lear. First Folio, 1623. [First Quarto and Folio texts have recently been argued to be distinct plays.]

The Tragedie of Macbeth. First Folio, 1623.

An Excellent conceited Tragedie of Romeo and Juliet. As it hath been often (with great applause) plaid publiquely, by the right Honourable the L. of Hunsdon his Servants. First Quarto, 1597. A "bad quarto."

The Most Excellent and lamentable Tragedie, of Romeo and Juliet. Newly corrected, augmented, and amended: As it hath bene sundry time publiquely acted, by the right Honourable the Lord Chamberlaine his Servants. Second Quarto, 1599.

The Tragedie of Romeo and Juliet. First Folio, 1623.

The Life of Tymon of Athens. First Folio, 1623.

The most Lamentable Romaine Tragedie of Titus Andronicus: As it was Plaide by the Right Honourable the Earle of Darbie, Earle of Pembrooke, and Earle of Sussex their Servants. First Quarto, 1594.

The Lamentable Tragedy of Titus Andronicus. First Folio, 1623.

Harbage, Alfred, general editor. *William Shakespeare: The Complete Works.* Pelican Text Revised. New York: The Viking Press, 1977. Modern edition most used for reference in this volume.

SECONDARY SOURCES

These sources are limited perforce to major books. The number of items in the *Shakespeare Quarterly* annual bibliography is now more than 3,600.

Adelman, Janet. *The Common Liar: An Essay on "Antony and Cleopatra."* New Haven and London: Yale University Press, 1973. Essay's groundwork: What constitutes meaning in a play? Effective thematic use of theoretical approach.

Barroll, J. Leeds. *Artificial Persons: The Formulation of Character in the Tragedies of Shakespeare.* Columbus: University of South Carolina Press, 1974. Questions Bradley's assumption about character, showing that it is not "real" in a modern sense. Erudite, but sometimes opaque in style.

Battenhouse, Roy W. *Shakespearean Tragedy: Its Art and Its Christian Premises.* Bloomington: Indiana University Press, 1969. Large book, finding religious defects in major characters. Some questionable judgments, but written thoughtfully by our most learned theological critic.

Bradley, A. C. *Shakespearean Tragedy: Lectures on "Hamlet," "Othello," "King Lear," and "Macbeth."* London: Macmillan, 1905. Classic early work on the "big four," treating mainly characters—to the disapproval of later critics. For its great influence on twentieth-century criticism and its varying fortunes, see Katherine Cooke, below.

Brooke, Nicholas. *Shakespeare's Early Tragedies.* London: Methuen, 1968. Primary aim is to rescue the early tragedies from teleological arguments that reduce them to immature anticipations of the later plays. Thoughtful and balanced, with equal attention to verbal and visual language. Early tragedies are seen as deeply skeptical.

Brower, Reuben A. *Hero and Saint: Shakespeare and the Graeco-Roman Heroic Tradition.* New York and Oxford: Oxford University Press, 1971. Parallels between pagan world and Shakespearean achievement. Main theme of the book is the "recognition of greatness." Heroic mode becomes saintly when pushed to extremes of suffering, endurance, self-knowledge. Hence, a classical complement to present study.

Campbell, Lily B. *Shakespeare's Tragic Heroes: Slaves of Passion*. Cambridge: Cambridge University Press, 1930. Learned, pioneering, but dated study of Elizabethan theories of the passions and their influences on *Hamlet, Othello, King Lear,* and *Macbeth*. The theories are still valuable as background, but the critical methodology is too confident, though more durably persuasive than many nonhistorical books.

Champion, Larry S. *Shakespeare's Tragic Perspective: The Development of His Dramatic Technique*. Athens: University of Georgia Press, 1975. Main concern is evolution of technique, concentrating on tragic pointers, character parallels and foils, analytic asides and soliloquies. Valuable for extensive references to secondary sources, but not critically distinguished.

Charlton, H. B. *Shakespearean Tragedy*. Cambridge: Cambridge University Press, 1948. Devoutly follows, with original thought, A. C. Bradley's method. Shakespeare's world is moral, not metaphysical; humanism and humanity hold Shakespeare more than theology. An important work.

Charney, Maurice. *Shakespeare's Roman Plays: The Function of Imagery in the Drama*. Cambridge: Harvard University Press, 1961. Language is only one source of imagery, which includes gestures, stage movements, and props, as well as words themselves. Influential and enduring study, though mainly for contribution of imagery; less so, but also a major work on the Roman plays.

Cooke, Katherine. *A. C. Bradley and His Influence in Twentieth-Century Shakespeare Criticism*. Oxford: Clarendon Press, 1972. Thorough and successful defense of *Shakespearean Tragedy* against later critics. Finds that there is a great mass of critics who cite Bradley for their purposes, but few who are willing to challenge him on his own terms.

Coursen, Herbert R., Jr. *Christian Ritual and the World of Shakespeare's Tragedies*. Lewisburg and London: Bucknell University Press and Associated University Presses, 1976. Hopes to show that sacrament, particularly the Eucharist, informs the distinct rhythm of each play and is central to an understanding of why these plays are tragedies. Essays a middle ground between allegory-hunters and those who see only dramatic statements of the human condition. Useful, but not always reliable, presentation of a religious background.

Cunningham, J. V. *Woe or Wonder: The Emotional Effect of Shakespearean Tragedy*. Denver: University of Denver Press, 1951. The "effect," arrived at from medieval and Renaissance philosophy and rhetoric, is one of fear, sorrow, and wonder. The basic text for this thesis is Donatus on Terence. The internal spring of plot is a willed act, or moral choice; the basic text for this principle of order is Averroes's paraphrase of Aristotle. This book is fragmentary, but useful and original. It also provides a good background for Edgar's "the art of known and feeling sorrows" stressed in the present study.

Danson, Lawrence. *Tragic Alphabet: Shakespeare's Drama of Language.* New Haven: Yale University Press, 1974. Main concern is linguistic inadequacy, *Titus,* for example, being a play about silence. Ritualized language has become debased and meaningless, and each play shows a different kind of linguistic failure. Original, but not centrally trustworthy about the meaning of tragedy.

Dickey, Franklin M. *Not Wisely But Too Well: Shakespeare's Love Tragedies.* San Marino, California: Huntington Library, 1957. A meticulously researched, but not openhearted book. Stresses, in the light of Renaissance theories of love and literary background, the "not wisely" of the title. But it judiciously rights the balance between the case for passionate love and the case for a wise, moral order. The most informed book on the love tragedies.

Elton, William R. *"King Lear" and the Gods.* San Marino, California: Huntington Library, 1966. Challenges the validity of the widespread "optimistic" view that *Lear* is a drama of meaningful suffering and redemption in a just universe. Useful not only as a critique of *Lear* but also as a massively researched view of Christian and pagan attitudes in the Renaissance. Only for so important a subject is the dense documentation justified. Not for bedside reading.

Evans, Bertrand. *Shakespeare's Tragic Practice.* Oxford and New York: Clarendon Press, 1979. Follows the masterly *Shakespeare's Comedies* (1960) in a study of the structures of the plays from the viewpoint of levels of awareness, though with more emphasis on the ways discrepancies of awareness are created. Despite some unorthodox judgments, necessitated by the approach, the book is still "about the tragedies primarily, and not about a dramatic device" (vii). Evans, as a critic of structure, must always be viewed with respect.

Farnham, Willard. *Shakespeare's Tragic Frontier: The World of His Final Tragedies.* Berkeley and Los Angeles: University of California Press, 1950. A judiciously researched and thought-out study of *Timon of Athens, Macbeth, Antony and Cleopatra,* and *Coriolanus,* whose characters live in a paradoxical world distinct from *King Lear* and earlier tragedies. Their nobility is one of life's mysteries, for it seems to issue from ignoble substance.

Frye, Northrop. *Fools of Time: Studies in Shakespeare's Tragedy.* Toronto: University of Toronto Press, 1967. This study has a threefold structure: tragedies of order, tragedies of passion, tragedies of isolation. Not Frye's best book, but uses his favorite and famous analytical devices in the archetypal figures he employs, such as Cain-figures, Absalom-figures, and order-figures.

Heilman, Robert B. *This Great Stage: Image and Structure in "King Lear."* Baton Rouge: Louisiana State University Press, 1948. Predecessor of pioneering imagistic methodology in his *Magic in the Web.* At first criticized but now recognized as a valuable total construct of words, ideas, and images. As in the following book, all the constituent metaphors are related to the large metaphor that is the play itself.

Holloway, John. *The Story of the Night: Studies in Shakespeare's Major Tragedies.* London: Routledge & Kegan Paul, 1961. Sets up "anthropological poetics." Creative process derives from archetypal mythmaking; tragedy is based on ritual of sacrifice or expulsion of scapegoat. Indebted to more pioneering critics like Northrop Frye but has independent ideas. Would be still better with broader scholarship.

Honigman, E. A. J. *Shakespeare: Seven Tragedies: The Dramatist's Manipulation of Response.* London: Macmillan; New York: Barnes and Noble, 1976. Asserts that Shakespeare was ingenious in the manipulation of his audience and artful in the control of their response. Focus limited to specific central issues: for example, the divided response produced by Brutus; or the audience sympathy with Hamlet's attitude toward and consciousness of his world. Attempts to reconstruct an imaginary audience devoid of time and place—hence, a venturesome undertaking.

Hunter, Robert G. *Shakespeare and the Mystery of God's Judgments.* Athens: University of Georgia Press, 1976. Hypothesis associates the making of Elizabethan tragedy with the new theology of the Protestant Reformation. If Luther and Calvin are right, tragic heroes are constrained. Hunter is a reliable authority, but tragic conclusions may be questioned.

Jorgensen, Paul A. *Lear's Self-Discovery.* Berkeley and Los Angeles: University of California's Press, 1967. Meaning and dramatic importance of self-discovery in Shakespeare's greatest depiction of the subject.

———.*Our Naked Frailties: Sensational Art and Meaning in "Macbeth."* Berkeley and Los Angeles: University of California Press, 1971. Aesthetics and the dramatic use of senses in the tragedy.

Knight, G. Wilson. *The Wheel of Fire: Interpretation of Shakespeare's Tragedies.* Cleveland and New York: The World Publishing Co., 1963. Knight's is an individual, poetic voice in modern interpretative, impressionistic criticism. His judgments are more interesting than persuasive. But he will be for a long time available in paperback. A beginning student should be wary of his interpetation of *Hamlet* and *Macbeth.*

Lawlor, John. *The Tragic Sense in Shakespeare.* London: Chatto & Windus, 1960. Attempts to assess in the world of the theater the relation between fate and free will. But throughout, the main focus is on paired opposites—its most interesting feature. Occasional thinness and flighty organization.

Long, Michael. *The Unnatural Scene: A Study in Shakespearean Tragedy.* London: Methuen, 1976. Rejects Schopenhauer and Nietzsche on tragedy, arguing for more precise, human characterizations. Rejects also "Shakespeare's tragic universe" approach. Discounts individual inconsistencies and character faults, sometimes putting all the blame on society. Overuse of sociological and psychological jargon. Chapter on *King Lear* is excellent.

Mack, Maynard. *"King Lear" in Our Time.* Berkeley and Los Angeles: University of California Press, 1965. A slender but significant volume, missing major impact only because it is "put together." Three approaches: aspects of stage history; sources, ranging from traditional literary ones to more archetypal; Mack's own notions of how the play speaks immediately to us today.

MacCallum, M. W. *Shakespeare's Roman Plays and Their Background.* London: Macmillan, 1910. For many years the most informative work on these plays. Examines Shakespeare's use of his sources and, especially, his transmutation of them. Sound but sometimes simple interpretations.

Marsh, Derick R. C. *Passion Lends Them Power: A Study of Shakespeare's Love Tragedies.* Manchester: Manchester University Press, 1976. A subtle study, balanced in drawing of links between love tragedies and love comedies. In *Antony and Cleopatra,* too much bias in favor of Cleopatra and too blunt denial (here and elsewhere) of the "reunion beyond the grave" motif. But he is far from alone in this denial.

McElroy, Bernard. *Shakespeare's Mature Tragedies.* Princeton: Princeton University Press, 1973. Confined to Bradley's "big four," although one can ask why *Hamlet* is a "mature" tragedy and *Antony and Cleopatra* is not. Acknowledges and ably utilizes Norman Rabkin's theory of "complementarities." (See Rabkin, below). Also, important concentration on the sense of unendurable loss.

McFarland, Thomas. *Tragic Meanings in Shakespeare.* New York: Random House, 1961. Valiant attempt, through philosophy, to find the "meanings,' but they remain difficult to pinpoint. The philosophical digressions are imperfectly integrated with the arguments and lead to simplistic pronouncements; for example, "Love is being; the world, non-being" (116).

Morris, Ivor. *Shakespeare's God: The Role of Religion in the Tragedies.* New York: St. Martin's Press, 1972. Attempts to locate an area of compatability between theology and drama. Weak on *Hamlet;* best chapters are on *Othello* and *Macbeth.*

Muir, Kenneth. *Shakespeare's Tragic Sequence.* London: Hutchinson University Library, 1972. Asserts that there is no such thing as Shakespearean tragedy: each play has its own form; each is an experiment in dramatic presentation of Shakespeare's necessary knowledge of life. Works written for the stage. Good introduction on recent criticism. A reasonable book.

Nevo, Ruth. *Tragic Form in Shakespeare.* Princeton: Princeton University Press, 1972. Disclaims "tragic theory" in favor of dramatic ordering of plot, character, etc. Nicely argued, but basic thesis is questionable: Shakespeare did not necessarily follow Aristotelian dramatic aesthetic.

Phillips, James E., Jr. *The State in Shakespeare's Greek and Roman Plays.* New York: Columbia University Press, 1940. Employs Renaissance political texts and theory to show the primary importance of the state in these plays. Learned and careful.

Proser, Matthew N. *The Heroic Image in Five Shakespearean Tragedies.* Princeton: Princeton University Press, 1965. Takes up Brutus, Othello, Macbeth, Antony, and Coriolanus. Tragedy ensues because of the discrepancy between the main character's self-conception and his full humanity as displayed in action. A subtle study.

Prosser, Eleanor. *Hamlet and Revenge.* Stanford: Stanford University Press, 1967. Historical review of Elizabethan ethical and dramatic codes and conventions. Challenges the assumed interpretations. For example, the Ghost is a devil seeking Hamlet's damnation. (He fails to do so). Wisely speculates on suitability of proposed interpretation for staging. Not for one-book beginners.

Quinn, Edward, James Ruoff, and Joseph Grennen. *The Major Shakespearean Tragedies: A Critical Bibliography.* New York: The Free Press; London: Collier-Macmillan Publishers, 1973. Not only much needed, this critical survey is also a model of its kind. Searching, responsible evaluations.

Rabkin, Norman. *Shakespeare and the Common Understanding.* New York: Macmillan Co., 1967. Defines Shakespeare's way of seeing, in a word taken from physicist Niels Bohr, as *complementarity:* "radically opposed and equally total commitments to the meaning of life coexist in a single harmonious vision" (14). Applies this pioneering approach to *Hamlet, Julius Caesar, Coriolanus,* and *Romeo and Juliet.* However stimulating, this approach should not be allowed to displace many others.

Ribner, Irving. *Patterns in Shakespearean Tragedy.* London: Methuen, 1960. Sees tragedy as "a product of man's desire to believe in a purposive ordered universe" (1). Shakespeare's art, based on medieval and Christian theories, is both symbolic and realistic. Salvation of characters is important. Book gives a thoughtful, welcome, but too easy view of the subject. One is, for example, happy to find suicides like Romeo and Othello redeemed, but theology makes it questionable. Less well received than his definitive volume on history plays.

Rosen, William. *Shakespeare and the Craft of Tragedy.* Cambridge: Harvard University Press, 1960. An elementary reading, one that gets at meaning through dramatic structure and technique. Studies *King Lear, Macbeth, Antony and Cleopatra,* and *Coriolanus.* Mainly secondary scholarship slighting Elizabethan worldview. Good on detail; slightly weaker on general synthesis.

Rosenberg, Marvin. *The Masks of "King Lear."* Berkeley and London: University of California Press, 1972. Like his comparable studies of *Othello* and *Macbeth,* this is a book making unparalleled use of actors and their point of view. Finds no one answer to what the play means or how it should be staged. Instead, uses musical, visual, rhetorical, mathematical, and other analogies. An awesomely researched and large book, bearing the author's unique stamps: independence of approach and a dramatic style.

Simmons, J. L. *Shakespeare's Pagan World. The Roman Tragedies.* Charlottesville: University Press of Virginia, 1973. "The antedating of Christian revelation is the most significant historical factor in these historical tragedies, and in this sense they are more genuinely Roman than is usually recognized" (8). Use of irony to develop Christian point of view. Book has most success when thesis is not dominant.

Skulsky, Harold. *Spirits Finely Touched: The Testing of Value and Integrity in Four Shakespearean Plays.* Athens: University of Georgia Press, 1976. Erudite and theoretically challenging but does not yield a central meaning. Too much dependence on patristic and scholastic philosophy; though this dependence is comprehensive and impessive, we should not be asked to measure what Hamlet says by Aquinas's logic.

Snyder, Susan. *The Comic Matrix of Shakespeare's Tragedies.* Princeton: Princeton University Press, 1979. Studies *Romeo and Juliet, Othello, Hamlet,* and *King Lear,* using the dramatic conventions of Shakespeare's own romantic comedies (up to 1595) as points of reference and departure. Comedy can shape tragedy. Comic characters can define the tragic situation by their very unawareness and irrelevance. An individual contribution by a critic who can also be a scholar.

Soellner, Rolf. *"Timon of Athens": Shakespeare's Pessimistic Tragedy.* Columbus: Ohio State University Press, 1979. Play seen as grounded in pessimistic intellectual tradition; so seen, it is as powerful as other plays of its era. Shakespeare succeeds in presenting misanthropy tragically as a plausible human experience. A much-needed book, and the author's respected scholarship should support much of its difficult doctrine.

Speaight, Robert. *Nature in Shakespearean Tragedy.* London: Hollis & Carter, 1955. "Nature" seen as everything given to man. The tragic moment is when comedy brings shape out of chaos and agreement out of conflict; tragedy is the catalyst of discord. Deals, sometimes perceptively, with *Hamlet, Macbeth, Othello, King Lear,* and *Antony and Cleopatra.*

Spivack, Bernard. *Shakespeare and the Allegory of Evil: The History of a Metaphor in Relation to His Major Villains.* New York: Columbia University Press, 1958. A major study of the development from allegory and the morality play of men like Edmund and Iago. Iago is persuasively seen as a "hybrid" figure, between abstract Vice of the morality play and a plausible reality. We must, Spivack contends, escape both naturalistic conventions of drama and romantic aesthetics. A large, learned, but readable book, sparked by wit.

Stampfer, Judah. *The Tragic Engagement: A Study of Shakespeare's Classical Tragedies.* New York: Funk & Wagnalls, 1968. "Tragic engagement" is *plot,* including "the engagement of a man with his entire gray zone" (10) (defined as texture, energies, and all that within a man that is not specifically characterization). Book suffers from vagueness, terms only loosely defined; for example, what is a "classical Shakespearean tragedy"? Some fine specific points, but these are widely interspersed.

Stirling, Brents. *Unity in Shakespearian Tragedy: The Interplay of Theme and Character.* New York: Columbia University Press, 1956. Addresses theme and its relation to structure and motivation. Structure is interconnection between elements or qualities; motivation is creation of a state of mind that governs not only a character but also his play. Most chapters first appeared as well-received articles; hence, doubtfulness of "Unity" in title. The ideas are keen, and the study of *Julius Caesar* in the present volume is indebted to "Or Else Were This a Savage Spectacle."

Traversi, Derek. *Shakespeare: The Roman Plays.* Stanford: Stanford University Press, 1963. Commentary similar to the reaction of an informed spectator. Definitely groups the three plays together, rating them on an equal level with the "big four." Imaginative, sometimes slow in interpretation, but reasoning is sound. Not strictly a pioneering study.

Waith, Eugene M. *The Herculean Hero in Marlowe, Chapman, Shakespeare, and Dryden.* New York: Columbia University Press, 1962. Valuable for this study principally in terms of Antony and Coriolanus. Defines for the first time a character type of great stature who is a danger, because of pride and anger, to society. A disciplined more than exciting study.

Whitaker, Virgil K. *The Mirror Up to Nature: The Technique of Shakespeare's Tragedies.* San Marino, California: Huntington Library, 1965. Emphasizes the need for interpreting tragedies in Christian terms. Central to Shakespeare's tragic technique are the crisis of moral choice (also found in this volume), the attempt to hold a mirror up to nature, and especially Hooker-based moral laws of nature and nations. Thoroughness and erudition impressive; for example, Whitaker reads and classifies one hundred tragedies of the age.

Wilson, J. Dover. *What Happens in "Hamlet."* Cambridge: Cambridge University Press, 1935. Scene-by-scene analysis, assuming that Shakespeare knew his business as a dramatist better than most critics did. Highly readable, but often boldly speculative. A milestone by a respected critic.

Index